CELEBRATE WITH CARDS!

CELEBRATE

WITH CARDS!

Dozens of Designs to Make for the Whole Family

LYNNE GARNER

 ST. MARTIN'S GRIFFIN

NEW YORK

www.stmartins.com

Text by **Lynne Garner**
Photographs by **Shona Wood**

Library of Congress Cataloging-in-Publication Data Available Upon Request

ISBN-10: 0-312-36705-8
ISBN-13: 978-0-312-36705-3

First U.S. Edition: October 2007

10 9 8 7 6 5 4 3 2 1

DEDICATION

FOR JON

I promise, no more card making—
well, not for a few days, anyway!

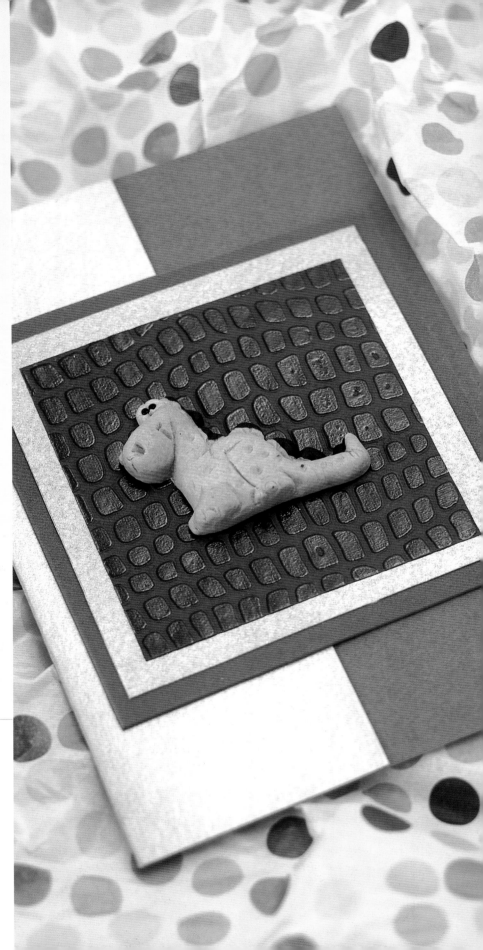

Contents

   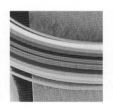  

Introduction

You may be surprised to learn that the oldest greetings card still in existence—a Valentine card now in The British Museum (London, England)—was written by Charles, Duke of Orleans, from his prison cell in 1415. Yet it was not until the 1800s, with the invention of new printing processes and the introduction of the Penny Post in England, in 1840, that the sending of greetings in the form of a card became popular and—just as importantly— affordable.

The first known published Christmas card appeared in London in 1843. The story is that Sir Henry Cole realized he had not left enough time to write all his normal greetings and therefore commissioned John Calcott Horsley to design a card for him. One thousand cards were printed and hand colored, only twelve of which are known to survive.

Soon other cards became popular, including birthday cards. However, the first birthday card was more of an apology than a birthday wish. At this time, it was customary on a person's birthday to visit them and wish them a good day—and the first birthday cards were sent as an apology for not being able to make a visit in person. Soon other occasions such as Easter, Halloween, and Thanksgiving were marked with a card.

During the Victorian era, many printers and artists took advantage of this new craze by starting up businesses printing mass-produced cards for all occasions.

For many years, America imported most of its greetings cards from England—although in

1849, a young woman named Ester Howland, from Massachusetts, was the first to publish Valentine cards. It was not until 1875, when a German immigrant named Louis Prang opened a lithographic store in Boston and started printing huge numbers of cards, that cards printed in the U.S. became widely available. In fact, Louis Prang is considered the father of the American Christmas card; by 1881, he was producing an incredible five million Christmas cards a year. His cards featured snow scenes, fireplaces, and children playing with toys and are now collected by people all over the world.

   Today, the sending of greetings has gone digital in the form of E-cards, E-greetings, and even Netograms (a short movie with a message attached)—yet people still love to send and receive traditional paper cards. Millions are sent each year and you can walk into any stationery store and find a whole array of beautiful cards to suit all ages and occasions. Nothing, however, quite beats the thrill of knowing that someone has taken the time and trouble to make a card especially for you. Equally, making a card for someone else gives you the opportunity to create something truly unique, that is tailored to suit the recipient.

   To inspire you to try it out yourself, we have packed this book with over fifty different designs for all kinds of occasions. By returning to the days when cards were made individually, by hand, you can show someone just how special they are.

Lynne Garner

Cardstock and paper

This section is a guide to the types of cardstock and paper you can use in this book. We have tried to feature as many different kinds as possible, but there are so many that you are sure to come across paper or cardstock that we have not had room to include.

HANDMADE PAPER

Although it is expensive compared with many other papers, handmade paper is a great medium to work with. Handmade papers come in a huge variety of thicknesses, textures, and colors and can contain decorations such as leaves and rose petals. You may experience problems when working with some handmade papers; for example, some glues may not adhere so well, so you may need to experiment.

SCRAPBOOKING PAPER

If you are a scrapbooker, then you'll know just how many different themes these decorative papers cover. They offer a wealth of ideas and are ideal for making large cards, as they tend to come in 12-in. (30-cm) square sheets.

WRAPPING PAPER

Commercially printed wrapping paper comes in all kinds of designs and is a great source of inspiration to any card maker. It often comes in large sheets or rolls, allowing you to create large numbers of cards at very little cost. One great way to use it is for 3-D découpage cards, as many designs contain repeated images.

BROWN PAPER

This is perhaps one of the most inexpensive papers that you can use in your card making, yet it offers many possibilities. For example, it looks great run through a paper crimper/ribbler, giving added depth to your card projects. Brown paper also looks fantastic mixed with flowers, feathers, twigs, and shells for natural-looking cards.

WALLPAPER

Just like wrapping paper, wallpaper can be a great source of inspiration. It can often be purchased quite cheaply, allowing you to create many, many cards on a budget.

SHEET MUSIC AND MAPS

Many of us have old maps and sheet music tucked away at the back of drawers or in the attic. Why not rescue them from their hiding place and use them as background papers?

NEWSPAPERS AND MAGAZINES

Both of these make ideal backing papers and offer a great way to recycle these often-neglected forms of paper.

PHOTOCOPIES AND SCANS

Photocopies and scans of photos, which you can print out from your home computer, are a great way of introducing something really individual to your card making. They give you the opportunity, among other things, to convert a photograph into a wonderful 3-D découpage image.

DOILIES

With their delicate cut edges, doilies can be attached to your card and integrated into the design. Alternatively, place one on your project and spray or sponge paint through it, in the same way as when using a stencil.

PAPER NAPKINS

Once upon a time napkins came in a single color and were, to be honest, extremely boring. Today, many companies manufacture themed party napkins and napkins especially for craft use.

QUILLING AND IRIS PAPERS

These are long thin strips of paper that come in a huge range of colors and in a variety of widths. They can be used as intended or woven, curled, and run though a paper crimper/ribbler.

TEABAG FOLDING PAPERS

Teabag folding papers are sheets of paper, often 12 x 8¼ in. (30 x 21 cm) in size, that contain squares of images repeated many times to fill the entire sheet. In addition to teabag-folded designs, they can be used as single motifs or to create 3-D découpage projects.

TRACING PAPER

A cheap alternative to parchment paper, tracing paper can be torn, pin pricked, and used to create wonderful layered effects. As with many craft materials, it has undergone a revolution in recent years, with many craft stores now offering it in an array of colors.

NON-GREASED BAKING PARCHMENT

Like tracing paper, this can be a cheap alternative to parchment paper and looks great torn, cut with decorative scissors, pin pricked, or embossed— although you need to take care with the latter two techniques, as non-greased baking parchment is not as forgiving as parchment paper.

PARCHMENT PAPER

Similar to tracing paper and non-greased baking parchment, parchment paper works well with techniques such as embossing and pin pricking, and allows you to create delicate-looking cards. However, it can be difficult to attach to a project as many types of glue show through this paper.

Decorative materials

The wonderful thing about card making is that you do not have to limit yourself to using just cardstock and paper. You can use a whole array of other items to decorate and enhance your projects. Here are just a few of the decorative materials that you can use; however, as your card making experience grows, you will discover your own.

BUTTONS
Buttons are available in many designs and can be fixed in place with glue, double-sided tape or foam pads, or sewn on with decorative thread.

SHELLS
Small shells and can be mixed with other natural found objects, such as feathers and leaves.

FEATHERS
The best way to attach a feather is to apply a thin line of glue down the center of the feather (the quill) or to sew it to the card by wrapping thread around the quill, at the base of the vane.

PRESSED FLOWERS
With the invention of the microwave flower press, drying flowers can be done in seconds. Alternatively, buy ready-made pressed flowers.

RIBBON AND LACE
These decorative materials are available at fabric and craft stores. Ribbons and lace with glue already on the back makes them easy to apply to most cardstock and paper surfaces.

BEADS
Beads can be made from bone, ceramic, plastic, glass, and metal. Attach them to greeting cards with double-sided self-adhesive foam pads (for flat beads), glue, or beading wire.

DECORATIVE CORD

Cord is widely available, with half a dozen or so toning shades on one card. Cord can be wrapped around a card or used to attach elements.

SKELETON LEAVES

Skeleton leaves give a delicate feel to your project and come in a wide variety of colors. The best way to attach them to cards is to use spray adhesive, as many other types of glue will seep to the front of the leaf and ruin your project.

CHARMS

Available individually or on themed sheets, charms can be attached using double-sided self-adhesive foam pads, hung on decorative cord, or threaded onto thin wire.

POLYMER CLAY

Polymer clay is a great craft material. It is easy to mold and comes in a range of colors that can be mixed together to create even more colors. To harden the clay, simply bake it in the oven, following the manufacturer's instructions.

AIR-DRY CLAY

Once available in just browns and reds, this kind of craft clay now comes in many colors and also in an extra-lightweight version, making it an ideal medium to work with. It can be modeled by hand or shaped in molds, allowing even the most heavy-handed of us to create fresh new designs.

BRADS

Brads can be used as decoration and to hold other embellishments in place. They are available in assorted shapes and colors, from circle or heart shapes to those topped with a diamanté.

EYELETS

Eyelets were traditionally used for leather items such as shoes, belts, and bags. They can be attached to cards using a simple hole-making tool and a hammer or a device with an ingenious ratchet mechanism.

EMBOSSING FOIL

Used in conjunction with a mat and an embossing tool, embossing foil can be used to create designs either freehand or using a stencil. It is easy to work with and can be mounted on a card to create an indented or a raised design.

INK PADS

There are two main types of ink pad. The first is known as dye ink. This is a fast-drying ink and is ideal for use with simple stamping. The second is pigment ink, which is a slow-drying ink suitable for use with embossing powder. If you are going to hand color stamped images with watercolor pencils, make sure you use a waterproof ink.

EMBOSSING POWDER

Embossing powder looks like glitter but melts when heat set and takes on a raised appearance.

Often used in conjunction with pigment ink, it comes in many grain sizes and colors.

CRAFT SAND

Another medium that has moved from the children's play room to the craft box is craft sand. The least messy way to apply it is to sprinkle it onto double-sided self-adhesive sheets.

GLITTER

Glitter can be attached using a variety of methods, including glue, double-sided tape, and double-sided self-adhesive sheets. Glitter glue pens are easier to use than loose glitter and glue.

FELT

Use felt to add texture. Before using it for the first time, test that the glue you are using does not seep through the felt and spoil its appearance.

FUN FOAM

Fun foam is available in plain colors as well as patterns such as animal prints. It is easy to cut and can be attached in a variety of ways, from gluing to attaching with brads or eyelets.

SHRINK PLASTIC

Shrink plastic can be drawn or stamped upon, and then shrunk in size using a heat gun. It is available in clear, opaque, and black versions. Some sheets are pre-sanded; others need to be sanded with a fine sandpaper before use.

PEEL 'N' STICKS AND STICKERS

These items are available in a massive range of themes and colors. Manufacturers have brought in a transfer sheet that allows you to use the parts of the sticker left behind after you have removed the main motif, so that nothing is wasted.

Craft tools

It is amazing how craft tools have evolved to give the card maker more and more scope for creating wonderfully crafted cards. Here are the basic tools that you may already have in your craft box or may wish to invest in.

CRAFT PUNCHES

Craft punches range from simple shapes such as circles to themed ones such as Santa or balloons. There are also border punches that allow you to create a continuous design, punches that allow you to weave with paper, and punches for decorating corners. Some punches not only punch out a design but also emboss at the same time, adding extra dimension to your projects.

DECORATIVE-EDGE SCISSORS

Zigzags, wavy lines, and scallop shapes are a few of the cuts you can make with decorative-edge scissors. Some new designs have inter-changeable blades or can be used to decorate corners. Some have four options on one blade.

EMBOSSING TOOL

An embossing tool has a fine metal rod that ends in a rounded tip at one or both ends. It can be used to draw along the lines of a stencil to create a raised effect on paper, cardstock, and embossing foil or used to trace or draw freehand designs onto parchment paper. You can also use an embossing tool in place of a bone folder to score fold lines onto cardstock.

LIGHT BOX

A light box is useful for embossing, as it allows you to see through the paper or card to the stencil below, making it easier to trace along the lines of the design. If you don't have a light box, use with masking tape and a closed window. Stick the stencil onto the glass, place the paper or cardstock on top, and emboss as normal.

HEAT GUN

You will need to use a heat gun when working with embossing powder, in order to melt and fuse the powder. Some heat guns look similar to a hair dryer, although they should never be used as such because of the amount of heat that they generate. A heat gun is also useful for drying inks and paints, and for melting wax when working on an encaustic wax project.

TEARING AIDS

Sometimes you may wish to tear paper or cardstock to create a decorative effect. You can tear against the edge of a ruler or use a special tool that you place on the paper and tear around to create torn pieces of paper or card to an exact shape and size.

PRICKING TOOL

A pricking tool is a pen-shaped device that ends in a sharp, needle-like point. There are also pricking tools that have two, three, or more pin heads, with some even arranged in a simple shape such as a semi-circle or a heart. If you do not have a pricking tool, then a needle fixed firmly into a cork will do the job just as well.

CARD-FOLDING BOARD

A card-folding board is a flat, grooved board which is used with an embossing tool or bone folder to create an indented line along which you can fold your cardstock in exactly the right position. It gives a "clean" fold, allowing you to create cards with a more professional finish.

RUBBER STAMP POSITIONER

When working with stamps that are on a wooden base, it is sometimes difficult to position them exactly where you want. As the name suggests, a stamp positioner enables you to place the stamp in exactly the right place, time and time again.

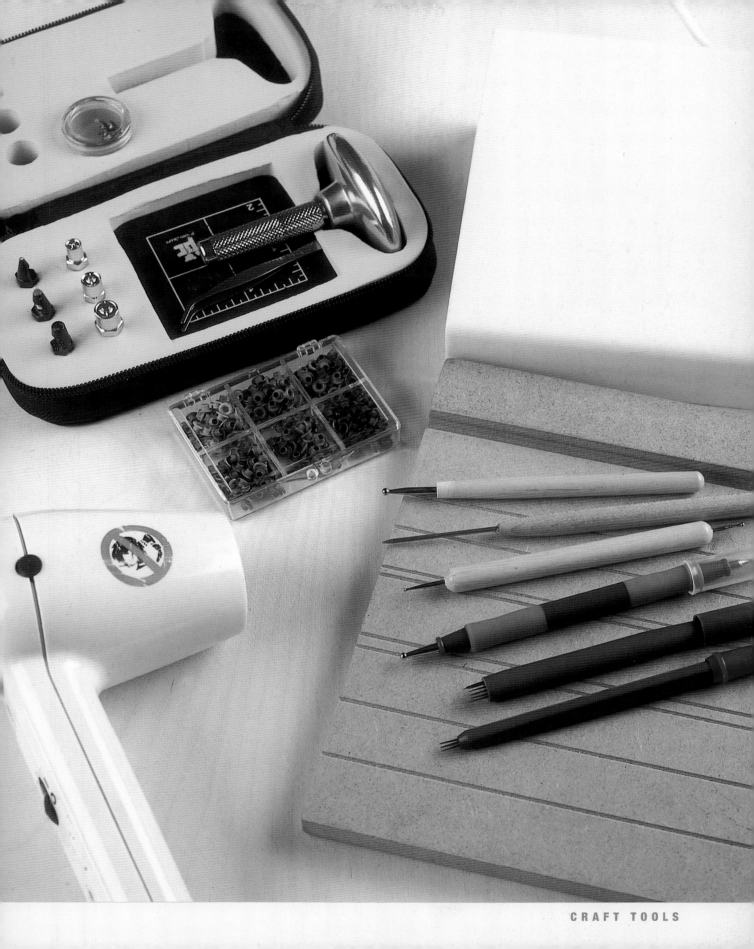

Cards and tags

Millions of cards are sold and sent each year, with messages ranging from love to happy birthday, from sympathy to sorry. So what better way to show your true feelings than by sending a handmade card? In this section we use a range of techniques including embossing, rubber stamping, découpage, quilling, and pop-ups, to name but a few. We have also included some tips to make your card making easier, along with variations to allow you to add your own personal touch to the cards you make. So don't lose precious card-making time: flip through the pages of this book, get making, and get giving!

New baby

Look what the stork has brought! To welcome a new baby into the world, here's a simple design featuring some delightful baby motifs embossed on pastel pink cardstock. Embossing is such an effective and professional-looking technique that the proud parents will never believe you made this card yourself.

YOU WILL NEED
8¼ x 6-in. (21 x 15-cm) sheet of pale pink marbled cardstock
Craft knife
Cutting mat
Ruler
Pencil
Light box
Embossing tool
Embossing stencil with stork and baby motifs
12 x 8¼-in. (30 x 21-cm) sheet of pink cardstock
Pink ink pad
Double-sided self-adhesive foam pads

1 Working on a cutting mat, trim ⅜ in. (1 cm) from one short and one long edge of the pink marble cardstock. Measure 1⅜ in. (3.5 cm) in from each short edge and 1¼ in. (3 cm) in from each long edge and draw a rectangle to these measurements. Cut out to give an aperture measuring 5⅛ x 3⅛ in. (13 x 8 cm).

2 Place the stencil on the light box, with the aperture card on top. Using an embossing tool, draw around small baby motifs of your choice, positioning them randomly.

3 Score and fold the pink cardstock in half to make the card blank. Open the card blank and emboss the stock motif centrally on the front. To help you position it correctly, place the stencil on the light box, with the aperture card on top, and the card blank on top of that.

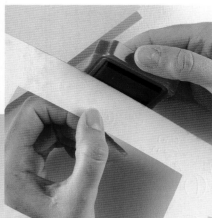

4 Remove the pieces of card from the light box and lightly stroke the pink ink pad around the edge of the aperture card.

5 Place double-sided self-adhesive foam pads on the back of the aperture card, line it up over the stork, and attach it to the front of the card.

For a traditional look, choose pink for a girl and blue for a boy!

top tips

- If you do not have a light box, tape the stencil to a closed window with a little low-tack masking tape.
- If the embossing tool sticks as you work, rub the tip over a piece of greased baking parchment. This will help it to run more smoothly.

Two little bundles of joy

The birth of twins is very special—so celebrate the occasion with this fun-to-make card. The cute baby motifs are made from polymer clay and a store-bought mold. The motifs are ever so simple to make, and will lend an interesting 3-D quality to your greeting cards.

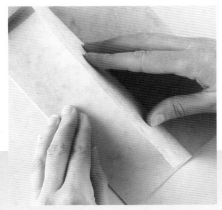

1 Fold the sheet of aquamarine cardstock in half, and then fold one long edge back to meet the first fold line. Crease sharply.

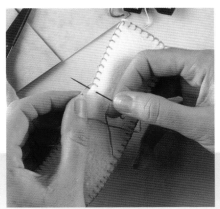

2 Cut two 2 x 8-in. (5 x 20-cm) pieces of white felt. Buttonhole stitch around the edge of one piece using light green embroidery floss and around the other piece using dark green embroidery floss.

3 Using spray adhesive, attach one piece of felt to the left of the card and the other to the right of the card.

Use the same technique to create a simple greeting card or matching gift tag for a single birth.

top tips

- *To make it easier to remove the motifs from the mold, place the mold in the freezer for ten minutes or so before you bake the clay, so the clay does not bend out of shape.*
- *To neaten the edges of your clay motif, pull back the sides of the mold a little before you push out the motif.*

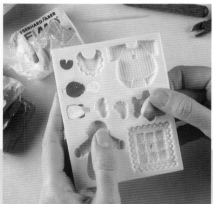

4 Using the mold, make up one set of four baby motifs using dark green polymer clay as the base, and one set using light green clay as the base. Use the toothpick to place two black seed beads on each teddy bear for the eyes.

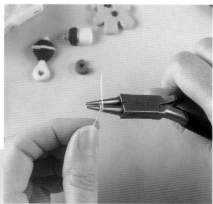

5 To make up the diaper pin, cut a short length of 22-gauge (0.6 mm) white wire, and wrap the center around the shaft of your round-nose pliers to form a complete loop, with both ends of the wire pointing in the same direction. Push both ends of wire into the clay. Bake all the clay motifs following the manufacturer's instructions.

6 Using a hot glue gun, stick the dark green motifs to the felt section edged with dark green embroidery floss, and the light green motifs to the light green felt section.

Vroom, vroom!

Boys love their toys, and this pop-up car card will be an instant hit with boys of all ages. By using the templates supplied, you'll find the card easier to make than you might imagine. We've given you two versions: one for a city slicker, the other for a boy racer!

YOU WILL NEED

Templates on pages 144–146

12 x 8¼-in. (30 x 21-cm) sheet of tan cardstock

12 x 8¼-in. (30 x 21-cm) sheet of black cardstock

8¼ x 6-in. (21 x 15-cm) sheet of blue cardstock

8¼ x 6-in. (21 x 15-cm) sheet of silver cardstock

12 x 8¼-in. (30 x 21-cm) sheet of blue marbled cardstock

Craft knife

Cutting mat

Ruler

Pencil

Craft glue

Black marker pen

Double-sided tape

Double-sided self-adhesive foam pads

For the "boy racer" in your life, change the car into a racing car and place it in front of a pile of tires. You'll find the template on page 146.

1 Begin by creating the car for the front of the card. Transfer the parts from the car template on page 144 onto cardstock of the appropriate color and cut out, minus the tabs on the wheels this time. (See our completed greeting card for color ideas.)

2 Glue the wheels, headlamps, and other details
onto the car body, and fix the windows behind.
Draw in the details with a black marker pen.

3 Transfer the road section and buildings templates on
pages 144–145 onto cardstock and cut out. Draw in
the windows with black marker pen. Fold the marbled
blue cardstock in half to make the card blank. Attach
the road sections to the base of the front of the card,
using double-sided tape. Attach the buildings, using
double-sided tape along the bottom edge and double-
sided self-adhesive foam pads along the top edge.

4 To complete the front of the card, attach the car
using double-sided self-adhesive foam pads.

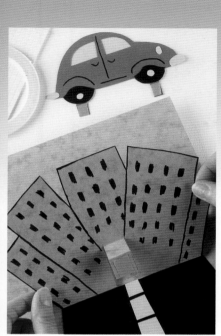

5 Now make the pop-up interior of the card.
Repeat Steps 1 and 2 to make a second
car, this time including the tabs on the
wheels. Transfer the road section and
buildings templates on pages 144–145
onto cardstock, add details in black marker
pen, and cut out. Cut and fold the tabs,
then attach the buildings and the road to
the interior of the card using plenty of
double-sided tape.

top tip

■ *To transfer the design lines of the wheel arches,
door handles and so forth, place the cut-out
shapes under the template, go over the lines
with an embossing tool, and then draw over the
embossed lines with a marker pen.*

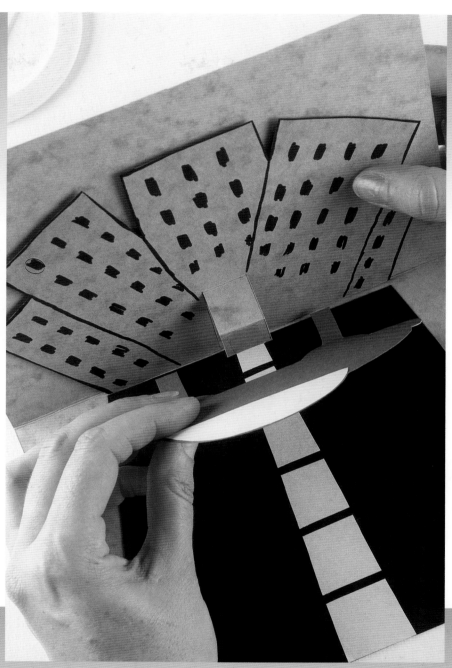

6 To attach the car, stick the tabs on the
wheels to the road, and the tab on the
building to the back of the car with double-
sided tape. Fold it flat, close the card, and
press firmly. The car will stick to the tab
and pop up each time the card is opened.

Jumbo in the jungle

This jolly little elephant card comes complete with its own box envelope. After the birthday celebrations are over, pop Jumbo back in his box where he makes a delightful framed picture for a child's bedroom. The elephant is simple to make because the head and body is all one color; use different colors to make a lion (opposite).

To make the card

YOU WILL NEED FOR THE CARD

12 x 8¼-in. (30 x 21-cm) sheet of tan cardstock

Craft knife

Cutting mat

Ruler

Pencil

Leaf embossing stencil on page 147

Light box

Embossing tool

8¼ x 6-in. (21 x 15-cm) sheet of thick light green paper

8¼ x 6-in. (21 x 15-cm) sheet of thick dark green paper

Gray polymer clay

Zoo life push mold

1 black seed bead

Toothpick

Double-sided self-adhesive foam pads

Hot glue gun

FOR THE BOX ENVELOPE

Templates on page 147

Two 12 x 8¼-in. (30 x 21-cm) sheets of tan cardstock

Double-sided tape

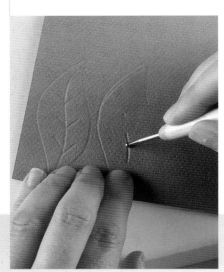

1 Cut a 10 x 5-in. (25 x 12.5-cm) piece of tan cardstock and fold it in half to make the card blank. Place the leaf embossing stencil from page 147 on a light box, and emboss five leaves on dark green paper and five on light green paper

2 Cut out the leaves. Apply a little craft glue to one end of each leaf and a self-adhesive foam pad to the other. Alternating light and dark green, attach the leaves around the outside of the card, overlapping and bending them slightly to create a subtle 3-D effect.

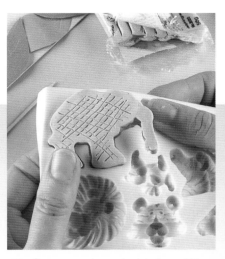

3 Press gray polymer clay into the mold to create the elephant.

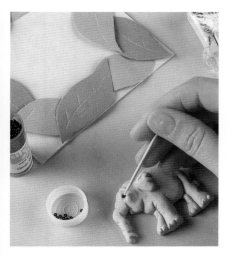

4 Add a black seed bead for the eye and bake following the manufacturer's instructions.

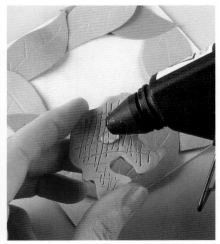

5 Using the glue gun, attach the elephant to the middle of the card.

top tip

■ *To ensure that the elephant sticks to the front of the greeting card, score the back with a craft tool prior to baking.*

To make the box envelope

1 Transfer the box base and lid templates on page 147 onto tan cardstock and cut out. Score along the fold lines, and then carefully cut out the shaped aperture.

2 Place the leaf embossing stencil on the light box, with the box lid on top, and begin to emboss the leaves, overlapping them. Where they overlap, do not stencil all of the leaf.

3 Place a small piece of double-sided tape on each tab of the box base and lid, fold in, and press to secure.

4 To complete, place the elephant card inside the box envelope.

top tips

- *When cutting out the window of the box envelope, cut each section in turn rather then trying to follow the line all the way around in one go. This will give you a cleaner cut.*
- *You can adapt the depth of the box to fit the depth of the clay motif that you are attaching to the front of your card.*
- *To add further interest to your card, cut around the outer edge of the leaves embossed around the front of the card.*
- *To protect your card further, attach a rectangle of acetate behind the window of the box envelope with double-sided tape.*

Layer a greeting card with handmade or textured papers and place a polymer-clay critter in the middle.

Flower power

Sometimes it's so difficult to find a birthday card and gift for a little girl, so why not make a card that turns into a birthday present? Once the big day has come and gone, simply detach the crimped section from the card and unwind the ribbon. The flower motif then becomes a pretty pendant necklace.

To make the pendant

YOU WILL NEED FOR THE PENDANT
2 blocks of polymer clay in complementary colors
Mini flower cookie cutter
7 seed beads
1¼-in. (3-cm) length 18-gauge (1 mm) silver wire
Wire cutters
Round-nose pliers

FOR THE CARD
8¼ x 6-in. (21 x 15-cm) sheet of embossed
   cardstock
8¼ x 6-in. (21 x 15-cm) tracing paper
Ruler
Double-sided tape
8¼ x 6-in. (21 x 15-cm) purple cardstock
Decorative-edge scissors
Paper crimper/ribbler
1 eyelet
Punch and eyelet setter
18-in. (45-cm) length of ⅛-in. (3-mm) wide
   ribbon complementary color
Double-sided self-adhesive foam pads

1 Cut a piece from the first block of polymer clay big enough to make a ball 1 in. (2.5 cm) across. Flatten the ball between your fingers and thumb, and press out a flower shape with the cookie cutter. Smooth the edges with your fingers.

2 Cut a smaller piece of polymer clay from the second block and roll it into a ball. Lightly press it centrally onto the first piece of clay to make the flower center.

3 Press the seed beads into the center of the flower design with your fingertips.

Adapt the color of the polymer clay and the ribbon to create a truly personal card and gift for the birthday girl.

4 Wrap a short length of wire around the shaft of your round-nose pliers to form a loop. Push the ends of the wire into the top of the pendant and bake following the manufacturer's instructions. Once baked, allow the pendant to cool before threading it onto the ribbon in Step 4 on page 31.

To make the card

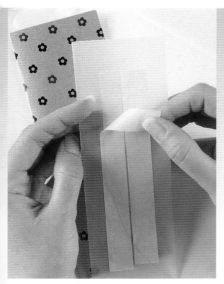

1 Fold the foil embossed card in half, long edge to long edge, to make the card blank. Tear the tracing paper slightly smaller than the card and mount it centrally, with the double-sided tape running down the middle of the card.

2 Using decorative-edge scissors, cut a piece of purple cardstock to 2 x 7 in. (5 x 18 cm) and run it through the paper crimper/ribbler.

3 Using the punch and eyelet setter, fix the eyelet in place about 1 in. (2.5 cm) down from the top of the crimped card, centered from side to side.

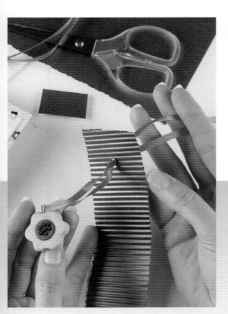

4 Thread the ribbon through the pendant loop, and then through the eyelet to the back of the crimped card.

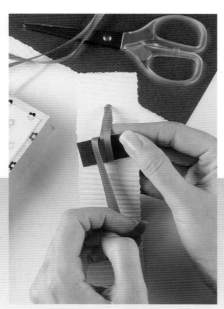

5 Wrap the ribbon around a small piece of cardstock and fix it securely to the back of the card with double-sided self-adhesive foam pads.

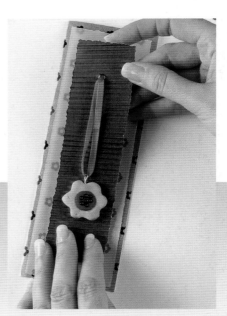

6 Attach the crimped card to the front of the card blank with more double-sided self-adhesive foam pads.

You're a star!

YOU WILL NEED

8¼ x 6-in. (21 x 15-cm) sheet of orange
  cardstock

6 x 4⅛-in. (15 x 10.5-cm) toning cardstock

Craft knife

Cutting mat

Ruler

Pencil

Decorative-edge scissors

Double-sided self-adhesive foam pads

Gold peel 'n' stick borders

Template on page 148

Sheet of felt in matching shade

Scissors

5 star-shaped studs

8¼ x 6 in. (21 x 15 cm) thin handmade paper in
  toning shade, with decorative pattern

Sewing thread

Needle

Narrow double-sided tape

Wide double-sided tape

Gold peel 'n' stick stars

If you know a little girl who dreams of being a prima ballerina, why not make this special, sparkly birthday card to let her know just how much of a star she is in your eyes?

The pretty skirt on the front of this greeting card is made from ultra-thin handmade paper.

1 Fold the orange cardstock in half to make the card blank. Using the decorative-edge scissors, trim the toning cardstock along all four edges, so that it's about ¼ in. (5 mm) smaller all around than the card blank. Attach the toning card to the front of the card blank using double-sided self-adhesive foam pads.

2 Attach gold peel 'n' stick borders along all
four edges of the trimmed card.

4 Place the star-shaped studs randomly over
the bodice and fix in place by pushing the
prongs through the felt and pressing them
down.

3 Transfer the bodice template on page 148
onto felt and cut out.

top tip

■ *Use double-sided tape to attach the felt, as craft glue may seep
through the felt and ruin the appearance of the finished card.*

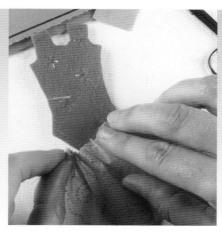

5 Cut a 7 x 2-in. (18 x 5-cm) strip of the decorated handmade paper. Sew running stitch along one long edge, then pull the thread so that it gathers the paper to 2¾ in. (6 cm) long.

6 Attach the gathered section to the back of the bodice along the bottom edge, using narrow double-sided tape.

7 Using wide double-sided tape, attach the bodice and skirt to the front of the card, positioning it diagonally from top right to bottom left.

8 Stick gold peel 'n' stick stars randomly around the dress, using the tip of your craft knife or a pair of long, thin tweezers for easy placement.

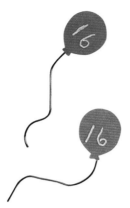

Sweet sixteen

In delicious shades of candy pink, with a scrumptious-looking pop-up birthday cake on the inside, this card is a sugar-sweet way to wish a young girl a happy sixteenth birthday. With the numbers left off the balloons, this makes a great card for anyone with a sweet tooth!

YOU WILL NEED

Two 12 x 8¼-in. (30 x 21-cm) sheets of pink cardstock

12 x 8¼ in. (30 x 21 cm) white craft netting

Scissors

4 pink paper fasteners

Templates on page 148

8¼ x 6-in. (21 x 15-cm) sheets of cardstock in various shades of pink

8¼ x 6-in. (21 x 15-cm) sheet of homemade sponged card in toning shade

Small piece of silver cardstock

Cutting mat

Craft knife

Ruler

Craft glue

Pink gel glitter pen

Balloon craft punch

Silver gel pen

26-gauge (0.4 mm) pink wire

Wire cutters

Double-sided self-adhesive foam pads

Double-sided tape

1 Fold one piece of pink cardstock in half to make the card blank. Cut a piece of craft netting slightly smaller than 8¼ x 6 in. (21 x 15 cm) and attach it to the front of the card blank using one pink paper fastener in each corner.

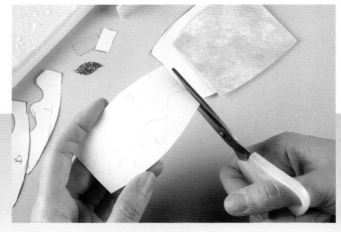

2 Transfer the pieces of the cake template on page 148 twice onto the appropriate colors of card, and cut out.

By mixing hand-painted papers, decorative craft papers, and plain cardstock, you can create a greeting card with great design interest.

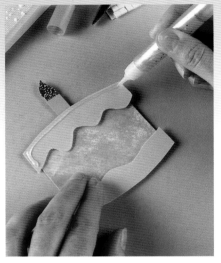

3 Assemble the two cakes, sticking the pieces in place with craft glue. Using the pink glitter pen, draw a line along the top and bottom edges of the cakes and leave to dry, preferably overnight.

4 Punch ten balloons from dark pink cardstock. Using a silver gel pen, write the number "16" on each one.

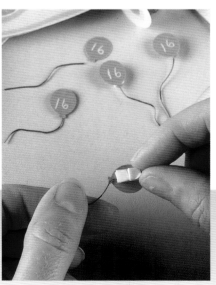

5 Cut ten pieces of pink wire about 2 in. (5 cm) long. Make a slight bend in each piece and attach one to the back of each balloon using double-sided self-adhesive foam pads.

6 Place double-sided self-adhesive foam pads to the back of one cake and five balloons, and attach them to the front of the card.

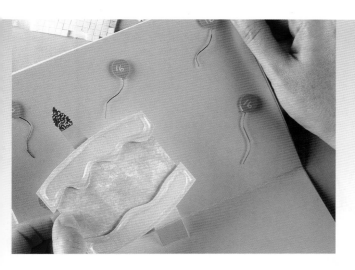

7 Take the second piece of pink cardstock and fold it in half. Trim ⅛ in. (3 mm) from one short side and one long side. Open out the card. Measure 4 in. (10 cm) in from each side, and cut a vertical slit ⅜ in. (1 cm) in length at these points, cutting across the center fold. Push the slit section inward to make a tab. Using double-sided tape, stick this card inside the first card. Attach the second cake to the tab, making sure the base of the cake does not stick out when the card is closed, and stick the remaining balloons in place to complete the card.

Why not draw a gift template to make a card with a cake on the outside and a pop-up surprise present on the inside?

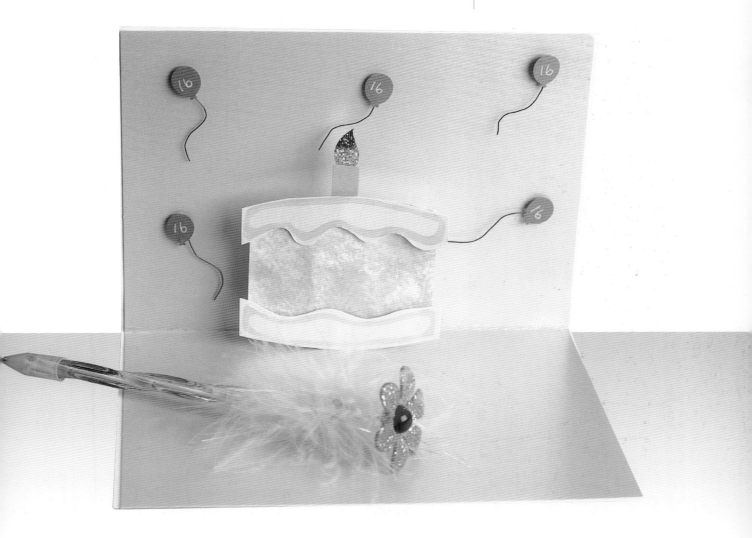

Pop!

Time to pop the champagne corks! With a shower of sparkling bubbles bursting out of the bottle, this is a great card for a landmark birthday, such as a 21st. This greeting card is given extra depth and interest thanks to the use of some simple folding and the addition of an array of tiny, sparkling beads.

YOU WILL NEED

8¼ x 6-in. (21 x 15-cm) sheet of cream marbled cardstock

Templates on page 149

12 x 8¼-in. (30 x 21-cm) sheet of tan marbled cardstock

6 x 4⅛-in. (15 x 10.5-cm) sheet of embossed or decorative paper

Scissors

Double-sided tape

Fine black pen

Silver gel pen

26-gauge (0.4 mm) gold wire

Wire cutters

Selection of small gold and orange beads

Round-nose pliers

Hot glue gun

Double-sided self-adhesive foam pads

1 Fold the cream cardstock in half, and then fold one long edge back to meet the first fold line. Crease sharply.

2 Transfer the bottle and cork templates on page 149 onto tan cardstock and the label onto embossed or decorative paper, and cut out. Attach the label to the bottle using double-sided tape.

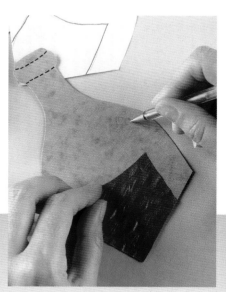

3 Following the template, add the detail to the bottle using a fine black pen and a silver gel pen.

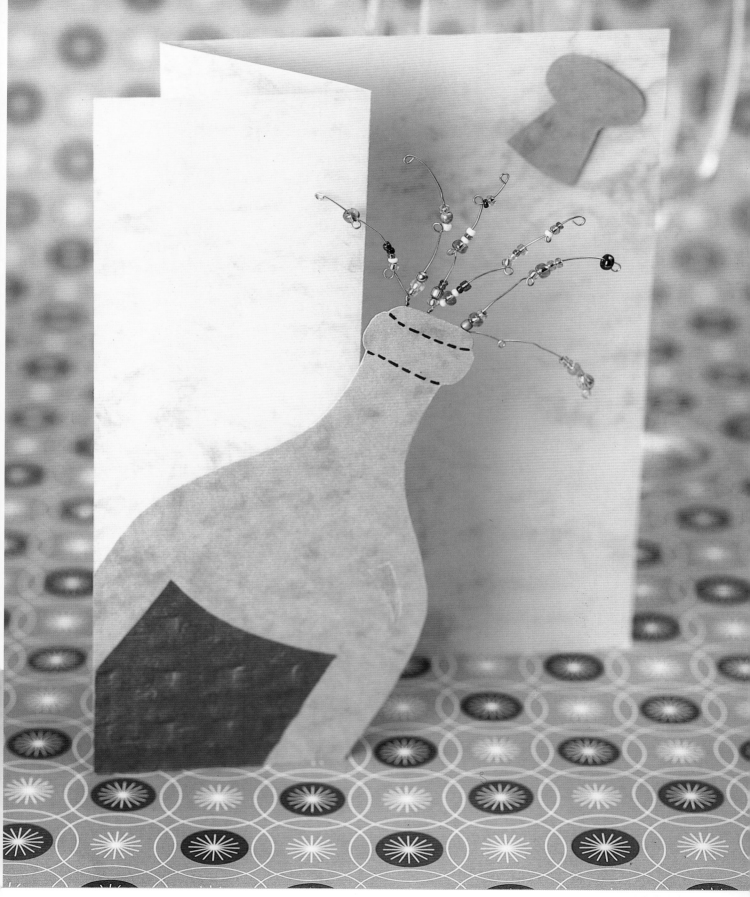

You could make a simple
beaded invitation in the same
style as the birthday card.

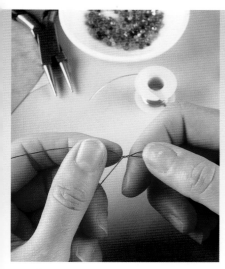

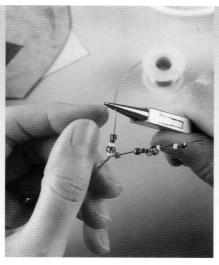

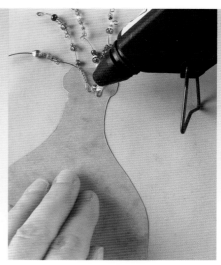

4 Cut three 6-in. (15-cm) lengths of 26-gauge (0.4 mm) gold wire. Fold each one in half, and twist the first ⅜ in. (1 cm) or so from the fold.

5 Thread a few beads onto one side of the wire, then wrap the wire around the shaft of your round-nose pliers to form a loop. Repeat the process along the length of the wire and on the other side of the wire. Do this with all three pieces, ending each wire with a small loop to prevent the beads from falling off.

6 Attach the beaded wires to the back of the bottle using a hot glue gun.

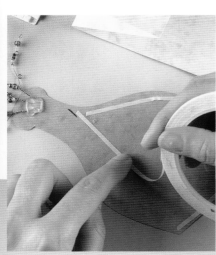

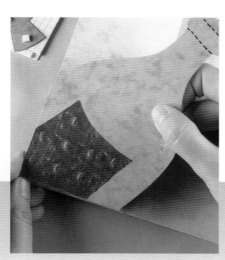

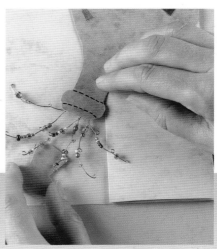

7 Align the bottle with the left-hand edge and base of the front of the card and mark where the bottle will overlap on the inside of the card. Place double-sided tape on the back of the bottle, making sure that you only apply it to the section that will be on the front of the greeting card.

8 Attach the bottle to the bottom left corner of the front of the card, aligning the straight edges.

9 Apply double-sided self-adhesive foam pads to the back of the cork. Close the card, work out the position of the cork, and attach it to the top right corner.

YOU WILL NEED

Two 12 x 8¼-in. (30 x 21-cm) sheets of matte
   silver cardstock
Musical manuscript parchment paper
12 x 8¼-in. (30 x 21-cm) sheet of musical
   manuscript paper
Craft glue
1-in. (2.5-cm) wide black organza ribbon
⅜-in. (1-cm) wide black satin ribbon
Musical note brads
Cutting mat
Craft knife
Ruler
Pencil
Double-sided tape

Life begins at 40

When a friend or family member reaches the ripe old
age of forty, sound a defiant fanfare and send this music-themed card
in celebration. We used a scrapbooking paper of musical notation for the
rosette in the center of the card, but if you can't find a suitable paper in
your local craft store, photocopy sheet music onto cream paper. You could
even incorporate the recipient's favorite song.

1 Fold one sheet of matte silver cardstock in
half to make the card blank. Tear the
musical manuscript parchment paper to
4 in. (10 cm) wide, and the remaining
sheet of matte silver cardstock to 2 in.
(5 cm) wide. Using double-sided tape,
layer these down the middle of the card
blank, applying tape only down the center
of the parchment paper so it will be hidden
when the next layer is stuck in place.

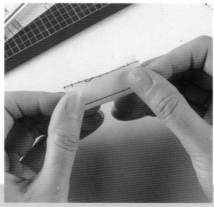

2 Cut eight 2-in. (5-cm) squares from the
musical manuscript paper. Take the first
square and, with the printed side on the
outside, fold it in half.

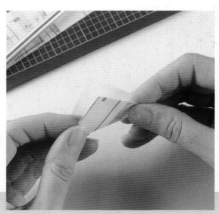

3 Unfold the square, and fold it in half again
from corner to corner, running your finger
along the fold to make a sharp crease.

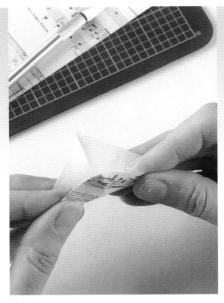

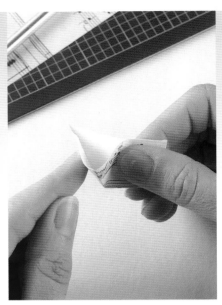

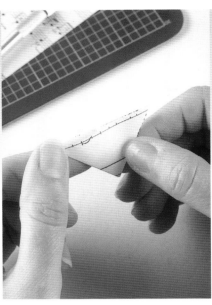

4 Unfold the square again, rotate it 90 degrees, and fold it again from corner to corner, making a sharp crease.

5 Unfold the square again and fold along the first crease line, with the print side still on the outside. Push the bottom left-hand corner up and in.

6 Repeat the process with the right-hand corner. Repeat Steps 2 through 6 with the other seven pieces of paper.

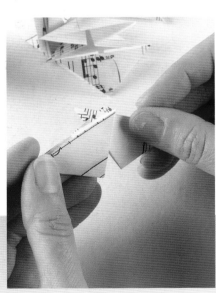

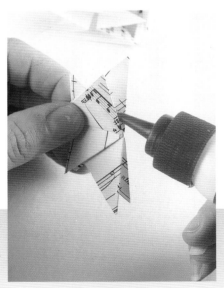

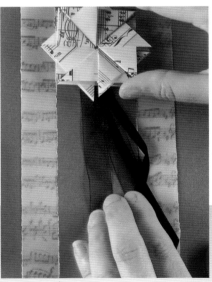

7 To create your teabag rosette, insert the points of the folded triangles under each other as shown.

8 Continue until you have completed the rosette, placing a tiny dab of craft glue between the fold of each triangle as you work to hold them in place.

9 Cut an 8-in. (20-cm) length of each ribbon, and fold in half. Using double-sided tape, attach the organza ribbon to the front of the card 2½ in. (5 cm) from the top and centered from side to side, with the satin ribbon on top. Trim the ends of the ribbon to fit then stick the teabag rosette on top.

10 Randomly position the musical note brads over the card, opening out the backs to hold in place.

Teabag folding can be used to create many different cards, such as this fun Christmas tree card. Make the bottom triangle out of a 2-in. (5-cm) square of paper, the second from a 1⅝-in. (4.5-cm) square, and the third from a 1½-in. (4-cm) square. Decorate with rows of sparkling beads.

top tips

■ *To improve the finish of your card, take a 12 x 8¼-in. (30 x 21-cm) piece of toning paper, trim ⅛ in. (3 mm) from one short and one long side, fold it in half, and stick it to the inside of the card to make an insert.*

■ *To insert the brads neatly, make a tiny hole through the front of the card using the tip of your craft knife.*

Sixty years young

For a truly memorable sixtieth birthday card, fill a card book full of photographs of the family and special occasions. Embellish the pages with ready-made charms and decorations along with things that mean something to the recipient, such as a pressed flower from their garden, a scrap of fabric left over from making a wedding dress, or a sticker that reflects their hobbies or work. You could also ask each family member to write a short personal message or poem on a piece of handmade paper.

YOU WILL NEED FOR THE BOOK
Large sheet of handmade paper
Water brush (or fine brush and pot of water)
Ruler
Pencil
Selection of photographs, approximately 1 x 2 in.
   (2 x 5 cm) in size
Double-sided tape
Craft knife
Cutting mat
Selection of buttons, charms, ribbon, and string
Eyelets or brads
Spray adhesive
8¼ x 6-in. (21 x 15-cm) sheet of black cardstock
Gold peel 'n' sticks
Needle and embroidery thread

FOR THE BOX
Two 12 x 8¼ in. (30 x 21 cm) sheets of black
   cardstock
Embossing tool or bone folder
Gold peel 'n' sticks

To make the book

1 Using the water brush (or a fine brush dipped in water), mark the handmade paper into four sections measuring 8 x 5 in. (20 x 12.5 cm). Place a ruler on the brushed lines and tear along the edge.

2 Cut out your chosen photographs, trimming them if necessary.

A personalized miniature album is both a
charming greeting card and a birthday
gift that the recipient will treasure.

3 Fold each section of handmade paper in half and begin to decorate with photographs, buttons, ribbon bows, and so on, making sure that the decorative elements do not go over the center fold.

4 Using spray adhesive, stick two pages back to back, aligning the center folds and sticking them down well.

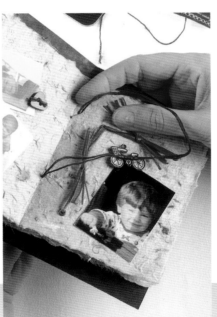

7 Turn the card over and tightly knot the embroidery thread to hold the pages in place. Cut off any excess.

5 Fold the black cardstock in half to make the card cover. Decorate the front corners and center with gold peel 'n' sticks. (To work out the middle, draw a faint pencil line from corner to corner.)

6 Place the pages inside the folded card cover. Thread the needle with an 8-in. (20-cm) length of embroidery thread. Make two holes along the fold line through all layers, and pull the thread through the holes, from the inside to the outside.

top tip

■ *Decorate each double-page spread as two separate halves using the photographs and decorative elements.*

To make the box

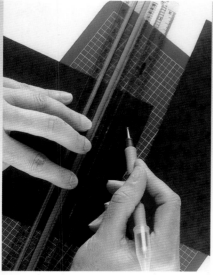

1 Cut a 5 x 6 ⅝-in. (12.5 x 17-cm) piece of black cardstock for the base, and a 5⅛ x 6¾-in. (12.7 x 17.2-cm) piece for the lid. On both pieces, score a line ⅝ in. (1.5 cm) in from the edge along all four sides, using an embossing tool or bone folder against the edge of a ruler.

2 On the base, score inward from each corner to the point where the side lines cross.

3 Fold along each of the side lines, and push the corners inward to create the base of the gift box.

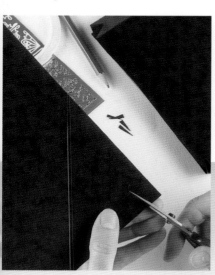

4 On the lid section, cut along one scored line at each corner and trim a sliver off the outer edge to make the tabs. Fold along each of the scored side lines, but do not stick them in place.

5 Decorate the lid of the box to match the front of the card.

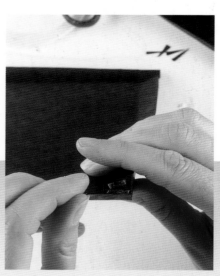

6 Apply a small piece of double-sided tape to each tab on both the lid and the base, fold it inward, and press to secure.

As an alternative to using bobbled paper, make your own marbled paper so you can match the colors with ease.

top tips

- *Before you stick the flowers onto the marbled paper, work out the positioning to ensure that they are evenly spaced.*
- *For a professional finish, line the card with a matching piece of paper.*

1 Lightly mark the center of one piece of red cardstock, then fold both sides in to this point to create a gatefold card blank. Using a craft knife and ruler on a cutting mat, trim to 6 in. (15 cm) square.

2 Using spray adhesive, glue the white bobble paper to the other piece of red cardstock and trim to 5 in. (12.5 cm) square. Cut a 4-in. (10-cm) square of marbled paper and attach it centrally to the white bobble paper.

100th birthday

A circlet of roses framed with velvet ribbon makes an elegant centerpiece. The key to this design is the use of beautifully toning colors and a simple pattern. This greeting card can easily be adapted to suit the recipient's tastes by using different paper flowers. Choose his or her favorite variety or select blooms to match the season of their birth.

YOU WILL NEED

Two 12 x 8¼-in. (30 x 21-cm) sheets of red
  cardstock
Craft knife
Cutting mat
Ruler
Pencil
Spray adhesive
8¼ x 6-in. (21 x 15-cm) sheet of white bobble
  specialty paper
8¼ x 6-in. (21 x 15-cm) sheet of homemade
  marbled paper
Double-sided tape
⅝-in. (1.5-cm) wide red velvet ribbon
Scissors
6 red paper roses
Craft glue

3 Using double-sided tape, attach red velvet ribbon around all four edges of the marbled paper, folding the ends around the back of the card for a neat finish.

4 Cut the stems off the roses, leaving a little wire at the base so the flowers do not fall apart. Arrange the flowers in a circle in the center of the marbled paper, and glue them in position with craft glue.

5 Position the decorated square centrally on the front of the card blank. Apply double-sided tape to the back, making sure that you apply it only to the part that will be on the left-hand flap of the card, and stick the decorated square in place.

Zodiac birthday

In this stylish project, an embossed silver zodiac motif is placed on a sparkling blue background reminiscent of the heavens at night—a quick and simple design for those occasions when you need to send a birthday greeting, but have very little time to make a card. In the Templates section, you will find designs for all twelve star signs.

YOU WILL NEED

8¼ x 6-in. (21 x 15-cm) sheet of silver cardstock
Craft knife
Cutting mat
Ruler
Pencil
8¼ x 6-in. (21 x 15-cm) sheet of dark blue glitter cardstock
Double-sided self-adhesive foam pads
Template on page 150
6 x 4⅛-in. (15 x 10.5-cm) sheet of embossing foil
Embossing mat
Embossing tool
Decorative-edge scissors

1 Cut a 4 x 8-in. (10 x 20-cm) piece of silver cardstock and fold it in half to make the card blank. Cut a 3¾-in. (9.5-cm) square of dark blue glitter cardstock and mount it centrally on the card blank, using double-sided self-adhesive foam pads.

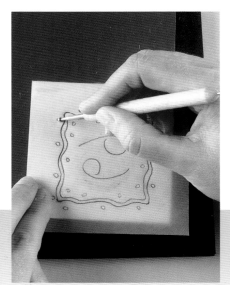

2 Select your design from the templates on page 150 and transfer it onto paper. Place the embossing foil on the embossing mat, with the template on top. Using the embossing tool, draw over the lines of the design to emboss it onto the foil.

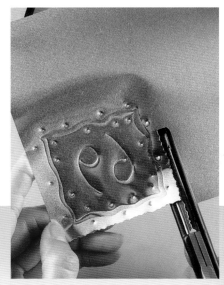

3 Using decorative-edge scissors, cut the embossed foil to 3½ in. (9 cm) square.

To make a matching gift tag, reduce the size of the design and mount it on matching cardstock. Pierce a hole in the top corner and thread with decorative embroidery thread.

4 Using double-sided self-adhesive foam pads, attach the embossed foil centrally to the front of the card

top tip

■ *To give your card a different finish to the one shown here, emboss part of the design then turn it over and emboss the remainder. The result will be a raised and indented design.*

Sorry it's late...

On occasions, time passes by so quickly that you can find you have missed someone's birthday. What better way to wish them a belated birthday than to send flowers? This pretty greeting card uses the traditional technique of quilling to create a floral bouquet, which is enhanced with tiny rhinestones and lacy parchment paper.

YOU WILL NEED

6 strips of ⅜-in. (10-mm) orange quilling paper
1 strip of ⅜-in. (10-mm) yellow quilling paper
7 strips of ⅛-in. (3-mm) yellow quilling paper
Small pair of fine-pointed scissors
Craft glue
Quilling tool
7 rhinestones approximately ⅛ in. (3 mm) in diameter
8¼ x 6-in. (21 x 15-cm) sheet of orange cardstock
8¼ x 6-in. (21 x 15-cm) sheet of yellow cardstock
Craft knife
Cutting mat
Ruler
Round craft punch 3¼ in. (8.5 cm) in diameter
Parchment paper or vellum
Spray adhesive
Toothpick
Double-sided tape

1 Using fine scissors, snip the ⅜-in. (10-mm) quilling papers every ⅛ in. (2–3 mm) along their length about half way in. Glue a ⅛-in. (3-mm) yellow quilling paper to the end of each strip, aligning it with the uncut edge of the wider quilling paper.

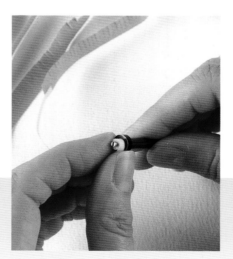

2 Place the end of the yellow ⅛-in. (3-mm) paper in the quilling tool and twirl it until you reach the end of the paper. Secure with a tiny dab of craft glue.

3 Using the tips of your fingers, gently "feather" out the quilled paper. Glue a rhinestone in the middle of each flower. Repeat Steps 1 through 3 to make six orange and one yellow flower.

Quilling strips come in different lengths. The length used in these flowers was 8⅝ in. (22 cm) for both widths of paper.

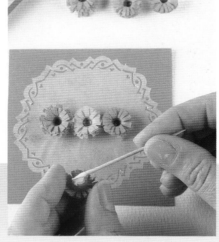

4   Cut a 3¾-in. (9.5-cm) square of orange cardstock and a 4⅛ x 8¼-in. (10.5 x 21-cm) piece of yellow cardstock. Fold the yellow cardstock in half to make the card blank. Punch a circle from the parchment paper or vellum, and mount it centrally on the orange card using spray adhesive.

5   Glue the quilled flowers to the parchment-paper circle, positioning the yellow flower in the center. Finally, attach the decorated orange card to the yellow card blank using double-sided tape.

top tips

- If you are worried that you will cut too far into the quilling paper and cut it in half, place ⅛ in. (3 mm) of the paper in the jaws of a bulldog clip; the clip will prevent you from cutting too far.
- When gluing small items such as these flowers, dip a wooden toothpick into the glue and then apply the glue to the item.

Sorry!

"Sorry" can be a very hard word to say, but regardless of the reason for having to say it—a missed appointment, forgetting someone's birthday or anniversary, making up after an argument—a handmade card can speak volumes. This contemporary card, with its abstract pattern of silver and black, is perfect for a note of apology.

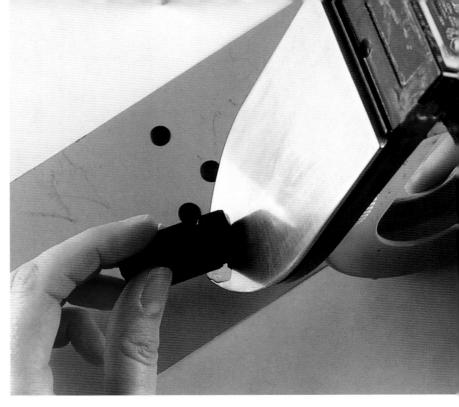

1 Holding the iron so the point of the base plate is just above the card, gently touch the silver and black wax onto the base plate and allow the wax to drip onto the silver wax painting cardstock.

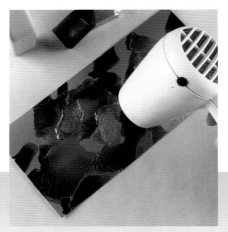

2 Heat with the heat gun, angling the gun so that the wax is blown across the card to create interesting patterns.

3 When the wax has dried hard, cut three 2-in. (5-cm) square sections from the wax-painted card and place double-sided self-adhesive foam pads on the back. Cut the 8¼ x 6-in. (21 x 15-cm) sheet of black cardstock to 3 x 7 in. (7.5 x 18 cm) and run it through the card crimper/ribbler.

top tip

■ *If you don't like the white line that appears around the outer edge of the waxed card when it is cut into sections, darken it with a black marker pen.*

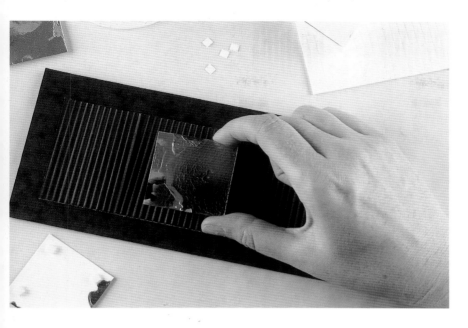

YOU WILL NEED

Scrap paper to protect your work surface

Black and silver wax blocks

Wax painting iron

8¼ x 6-in. (21 x 15-cm) sheet of silver wax
    painting cardstock

Heat gun

8¼ x 6-in. (21 x 15-cm) sheet of black cardstock

Paper crimper/ribbler

12 x 8¼-in. (30 x 21-cm) sheet of black cardstock

Ruler

Craft knife

Cutting mat

Double-sided tape

Double-sided self-adhesive foam pads

4 Cut the larger sheet of black cardstock to 8 x 8¼ in. (20 x 21 cm) and fold it in half to make the card blank. Using double-sided tape, center the ribbled card on the card blank, and stick the ribbled card in place with double-sided self-adhesive foam pads. Place the three wax sections on top, spacing them evenly.

The square card in the photograph (right) was made from the off-cuts of the main card and decorated with silver peel 'n' stick strips.

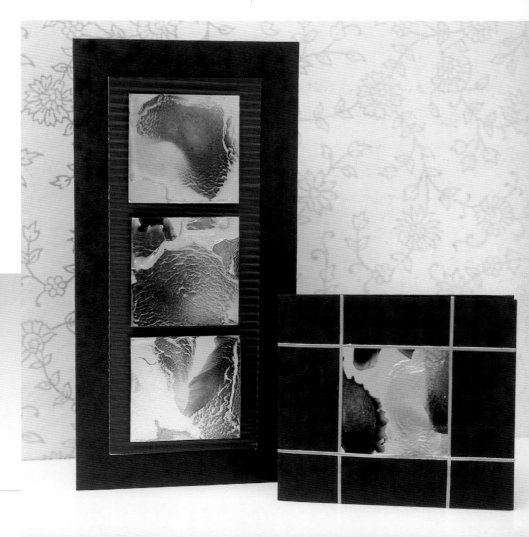

Congratulations

A red heart and rose-petal paper—what could be more appropriate for a card celebrating a declaration of love? With its simply shaped wire motif and bold color scheme, this engagement card has a very contemporary feel. It would work equally well as a Valentine card.

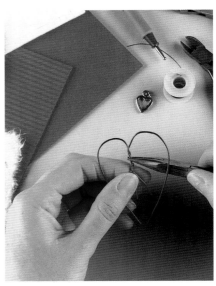

2 Cut a 9-in. (23-cm) length of 18-gauge (1 mm) red wire and form it into a heart shape, twisting the wires in the center of the heart together.

YOU WILL NEED

12 x 8¼-in. (30 x 21-cm) sheet of red cardstock
Craft knife
Cutting mat
Ruler
Water brush (or fine brush and pot of water)
Paper crimper/ribbler
6 x 4⅛-in. (15 x 10.5-cm) sheet of handmade
    paper with petals
18-gauge (1 mm) red wire
Wire cutters
Round-nose pliers
Heart charm
26-gauge (0.4 mm) red wire
Pricking tool
Double-sided self-adhesive foam pads
Double-sided tape

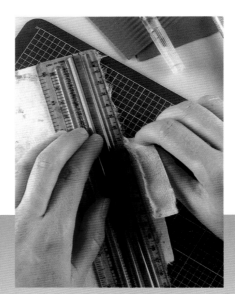

1 Cut the red cardstock in half and fold one piece in half. Cut the other piece to 3 x 5 in. (7.5 x 12.5 cm) and run it through the paper crimper/ribbler. Tear the handmade paper to slightly smaller than the ribbled card. (To make it easier to tear, first brush with water to soften the paper fibers.)

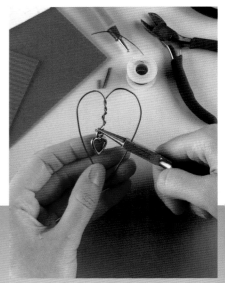

3 Attach the heart charm to the end of the twisted wires, then bend the ends of the wires into a loop using the tips of your round-nose pliers.

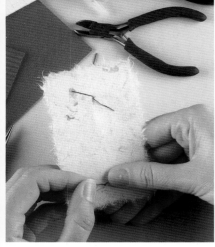

4 Place the heart on the handmade paper. Using a pricking tool, make two tiny holes through the paper—one at the top of the heart and one at the bottom. Cut two 2-in. (5-cm) lengths of 26-gauge (0.4 mm) red wire, and bend them in half. Loop them over the edge of the heart and push both ends of wire through the hole. Twist the wires together on the back of the paper to secure, then cut off any excess.

To make a gatefold card (below right), attach a simple wire heart to some handmade paper, then attach the paper to the left-hand flap of the card blank.

top tip

■ *If your handmade paper is thin and you are worried that it may tear when you attach the heart, first mount it on thin cardstock with spray adhesive.*

5 Center the ribbled card on the front of the card blank, and stick in place with double-sided self-adhesive foam pads. Center the handmade paper on top, and fix in place with double-sided tape.

Wedding bells

There are few sounds more joyous than a peal of bells announcing that a wedding is taking place. Here, we've given an embossed bell motif an unusual twist by transforming it into a shaker card of glistening, jewel-like micro beads. Choose embossing powder and micro beads to match the color theme of the wedding.

YOU WILL NEED

- 8¼ x 6-in. (21 x 15-cm) sheet of purple cardstock
- 6 x 4⅛-in. (15 x 10.5-cm) sheet of cream cardstock
- Decorative-edge scissors
- Clear embossing ink
- Rubber wedding-bell stamp
- Lilac embossing powder
- Heat gun
- Craft knife
- Cutting mat
- Ruler
- Acetate
- Double-sided self-adhesive foam tape
- Lilac glitter or micro beads
- Narrow double-sided tape

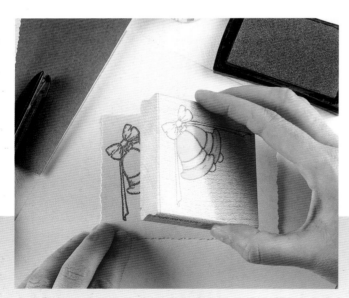

1 Fold the purple cardstock in half to make the card blank. Trim around the edges of the cream cardstock using decorative-edge scissors. Using clear embossing ink, stamp your image in the top left corner.

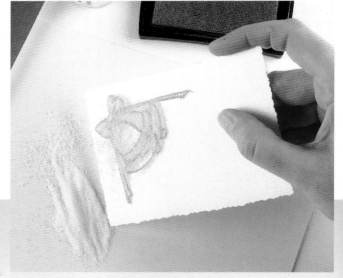

2 Sprinkle over the embossing powder, shake off any excess, and heat with the heat gun until the powder fuses.

For a quick-and-easy card, stamp the image, mount it on toning handmade paper, then mount the handmade paper on the front of the card.

3 Using a craft knife, cut out the interior of the bell. Cut a piece of acetate slightly larger than the cut-out area. Attach it to the back of the card using double-sided tape.

4 Place double-sided self-adhesive foam tape in a rectangle around the cut-out area, with smaller pieces of tape around the edges of the cream card. Sprinkle lilac glitter or micro beads into the rectangle, filling about one-third of the area.

5 Peel off the backing paper from the double-sided foam tape, lower the card blank onto it, aligning it carefully, and press gently to secure.

top tip

■ *If you feel you will not be able to line up the card accurately in Step 5, open out the folded card blank and make a small pile of beads near the top left, making sure they fit within the area that will be covered by the acetate window. Carefully lower the stamped card onto the card blank, and press gently all around the edges and the aperture to fix it in place.*

6 Turn the card over. Apply two strips of narrow double-sided tape down the right-hand side of the card and sprinkle with lilac glitter or micro beads. Shake off any excess.

Use a computer to add a filter effect to the photograph and give an artistic finish to your greeting card.

Happy anniversary

For a truly unique anniversary card, incorporate a photo of the happy couple. In this card, we've combined one of the oldest papercrafting techniques—3-D découpage—with the very latest computer technology to transform a favorite photo into a work of art, but you could use an unmanipulated photo if you prefer.

YOU WILL NEED

12 x 8¼-in. (30 x 21-cm) sheet of bronze
    cardstock

8¼ x 6-in. (21 x 15-cm) sheet of handmade paper

Water brush (or fine brush and pot of water)

Small pair of fine pointed scissors

4 copies of one 5½ x 4-in. (14 x 10-cm)
    photograph

3 x 1¼ x 1-in. (3 x 2.5-cm) copies of the main
    photograph

Double-sided tape

Double-sided self-adhesive foam pads

Craft knife

Ruler

8¼ x 6-in. (21 x 15-cm) sheet of bronze cardstock

Paper crimper/ribbler

1   Fold the large sheet of bronze cardstock in half to make the card blank. Tear the handmade paper to slightly smaller than the folded card blank and attach it centrally to the front, using double-sided tape. (To make it easier to tear, brush the area you want to tear with water, to soften the paper fibers.)

2 Cut the four copies of the large photograph into different sections, so that you can layer them to create a 3-D effect.

3 Attach the first photo to the left-hand side of the card blank using double-sided tape. Then build up the subsequent layers using double-sided self-adhesive foam pads

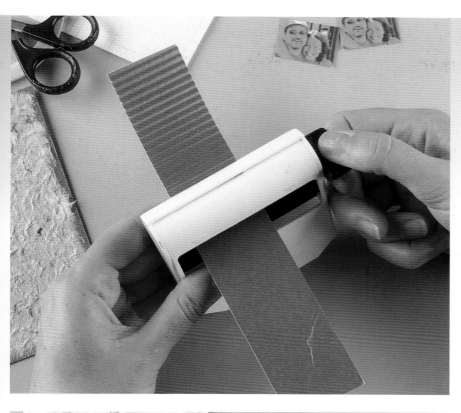

4 Cut a 6 x 1½-in. (15 x 4-cm) strip of bronze cardstock, run it through the paper crimper/ribbler, and attach it to the right-hand side of the card using self-adhesive foam pads.

5 Stick the three small photographs centrally down the strip of ribbled card to finish

■ *When cutting out your photographs, work from the back layer to the front. This will help you to work out which element should be removed with each new layer.*

Gone fishing

A divorce is always a sad time, but a handmade card will remind your friends that you are there for them if they need you. This tongue-in-cheek card is a reminder for anyone who's newly divorced that there are, as the saying goes, "plenty more fish in the sea!"

YOU WILL NEED

Scrap paper to cover work surface

Double-sided self-adhesive sheet

6 x 4⅛-in. (15 x 10.5-cm) sheet of cream cardstock

Black outline fish- and shell-themed stickers

Colored craft sand

Small spoon

Scissors

Pencil

8¼ x 6-in. (21 x 15-cm) sheet of pale green cardstock

6 x 4⅛-in. (15 x 10.5-cm) sheet of toning handmade paper

Spray adhesive

Double-sided self-adhesive foam pads

Handmade paper and colored sand lend a wonderful texture to a simple card base.

To create a less symmetrical look, cut away some of the front of the card using the edges of the sticker as the design line.

1 Remove one side of the protective cover from the double-sided sticky sheet and stick it over the cream cardstock.

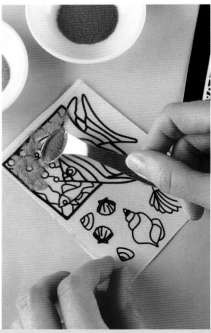

2 Remove the second side of the protective cover and attach the black outline stickers, taking care not to stretch them out of shape.

3 Using a spoon, begin to sprinkle on the craft sand, one color at time.

4 Leave any excess sand as you add the other colors. When the image is completely covered, press the sand down with your fingertips to make sure that it has stuck all over, then shake off any excess.

5 Carefully cut around each section of the design, taking care to cut just outside the black stickers.

6 Fold the pale green cardstock in half to make the card blank. Using spray adhesive, attach the handmade paper to the front. Attach the sand-covered sticker designs to the front of your card using double-sided self-adhesive foam pads.

In sympathy

A card and a message of support mean so much to anyone who has suffered a bereavement. When it is almost impossible to find the right words, a beautiful handmade card will show just how much you care. Pin pricking and embossing create a delicate effect that's subtly appropriate for such a thoughtful greeting card.

YOU WILL NEED

8¼ x 6-in. (21 x 15-cm) sheet of parchment paper
Ruler
Pencil
Pricking mat
Semi-circular pricking tool
Template on page 151
Embossing mat
Embossing tool
12 x 8¼-in. (30 x 21-cm) sheet of purple cardstock
4 small silver split pins

1 Tear the parchment paper to 7 x 5 in. (18 x 12.5 cm). Place it on the pricking mat and prick two rows of semi-circles around all four edges.

2 Make a copy of the template on page 151. Place it on the embossing mat with the parchment on top, making sure that the dove is in the center. Gently trace over the image with the embossing tool.

3 Fold the purple cardstock in half to make the card blank. Center the decorated parchment paper on the front of the card and, using the tip of the pricking tool, make four holes, one in each corner. Fix the parchment in place using the four silver split pins.

top tip

■ *To avoid getting your hands into awkward positions as you*
emboss, move the embossing mat and the design around
while holding the embossing tool on the design to prevent
it from slipping out of position.

Passed with flying colors!

After years of study, graduation day has finally arrived. To congratulate a hard-working student on his or her achievement, why not send this very special handmade card? You can change the color of the ribbon and tassel to match their faculty colors.

YOU WILL NEED

12 x 8¼-in. (30 x 21-cm) sheet of black cardstock
One sheet of black fun foam
Scissors
Pencil
Template on page 151
White 3-D fabric paint
28-gauge (0.3 mm) black wire
Wire cutters
Small white tassel
6 x 4⅛-in. (15 x 10.5-cm) sheet of parchment
    paper
Pricking mat
Semi-circular pricking tool
⅜-in. (1-cm)-wide purple organza ribbon
1-in. (2.5-cm)-wide purple satin ribbon
Scissors
Double-sided tape

1 Fold the black cardstock in half to make the card blank. Transfer the template on page 151 onto the fun foam. Cut out the mortarboard design, and outline it using the 3-D fabric paint. Leave to dry, preferably overnight.

2 Pierce a small hole in the center of the mortarboard. Cut a small length of 28-gauge (0.3 mm) black wire and thread it through the loop at the top of the tassel. Push both ends of the wire through the hole, and twist both ends together on the reverse to secure.

3 Place the parchment paper on the pricking mat and prick three rows of semi-circular holes around the outside.

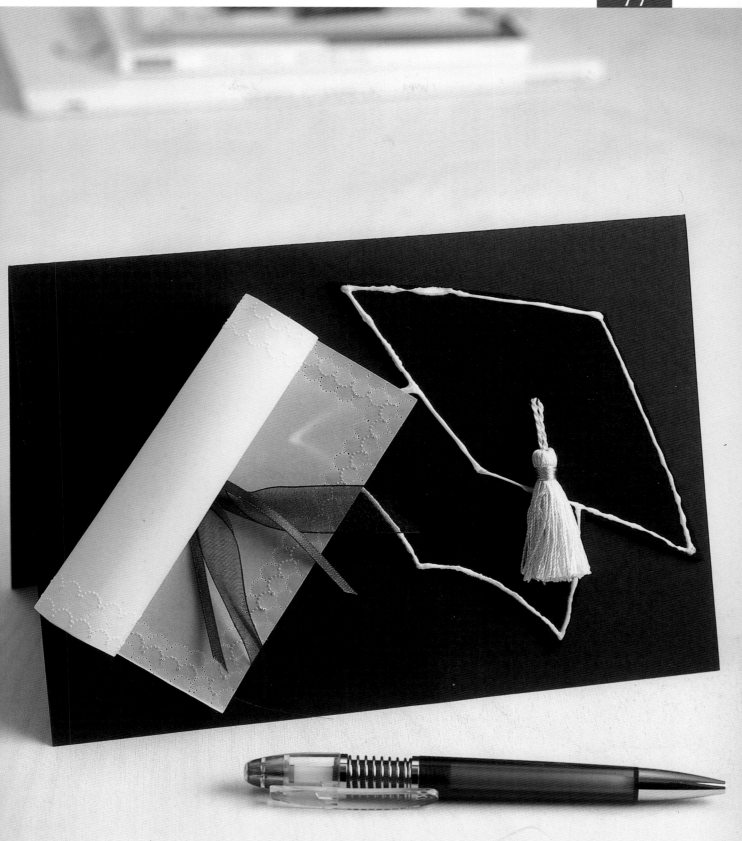

Turning the card around and choosing marbled paper for the base card, creates a completely different look.

4 Cut a 6-in. (15-cm) length of each ribbon, knot them together in the center, and trim the ends into a V-shape. Fold in half and, using a little double-sided tape, stick them along one short edge of the parchment paper, about 1 in. (2.5 cm) from the edge.

5 Place double-sided tape across the width of the paper at the same height. Roll the paper until you reach the sticky tape, then press gently to secure the scroll.

top tips

■ To add interest, prick one row on one side of the parchment paper, then turn the paper over and prick from the other side. Doing this will create a row of smooth holes and a row of raised holes.

■ To save time, don't prick the second short edge of the parchment paper, as this will not be seen once the paper has been rolled.

6 Using double-sided tape, attach the mortarboard to the right of the base card and the scroll to the left.

Welcome to your new home

Send your warmest wishes for a happy new home with this delightful pop-up card. The bright colors and naïve style are reminiscent of a child's drawing, and add to the sense of fun. The combination of embossing and handmade paper adds depth, too. A handmade envelope completes the gift.

YOU WILL NEED

12 x 8¼-in. (30 x 21-cm) sheet of brown cardstock
Brick-textured embossing plate
Embossing tool
Templates on page 152
Pencil
8¼ x 6-in. (21 x 15-cm) sheet of black cardstock
12 x 8¼-in. (30 x 21-cm) sheet of orange cardstock
Craft knife
Cutting mat
Ruler
Black marker pen
Double-sided tape
Double-sided self-adhesive foam pads
16½ x 12-in. (42 x 30-cm) sheet of white handmade paper with inclusions
Water brush (or fine brush and pot of water)
Small pair of scissors

To make the card

1 Place the brown cardstock on the brick embossing plate and, using the embossing tool, emboss enough of the brick design to make two house shapes.

2 Cut the orange cardstock in half and
reserve one piece to make the card blank in
Step 6. Transfer the templates on page 152
twice onto cardstock of the appropriate
colors, then cut out each element of the
two houses. Cut out two slightly smaller
house shapes in black for use in Step 4.

3 Outline the various sections of the two
houses using the black marker pen, and
draw on the details such as the door
handles and roof tiles.

4 Stick the orange curtains behind the
windows using double-sided tape, then
place the black section behind them. Attach
the other sections of the two houses using
more double-sided tape.

5   Tear a piece of handmade paper to 5 in.
    (12.5 cm) square. (To make it easier to tear,
    brush the area you want to tear with water,
    to soften the paper fibers.)

6   Fold the reserved orange cardstock in half
    to make the card blank, then attach the torn
    handmade paper using double-sided tape.

7 With the fold of the card running along the top edge, attach the house centrally to the front of the card using double-sided self-adhesive foam pads.

8 Tear a second piece of handmade paper to 5 x 10¾ in. (12.5 x 27.5 cm), and attach it to the inside of the card with double-sided tape. Cut a 2½ x 1¼-in. (6 x 3-cm) piece of orange cardstock, and fold it into four equal parts to make the tab. Attach it centrally along the fold of the card. Using double-sided tape, attach the second house to the tab, so that it pops up when the card is opened, making sure that the house does not stick out when the card is closed.

top tip

■ *To write a message, cut a 3-in. (7.5-cm) square of card and attach it to the inside of the card, in front of the house.*

To make the envelope

1 Cut a 9½-in. (24-cm) square of the remaining handmade paper. From one corner, measure 5 in. (12.5 cm) along one edge, and then 5 in. (12.5 cm) along the adjoining edge. Fold the corner inward between these two points. Repeat on the opposite side of the square.

2 Place a strip of double-sided tape along the lower edge of each folded-in corner. Bring up the bottom corner to overlap the folded-in sections slightly and stick down. Slip in the card and seal the envelope

Sorry you're leaving

YOU WILL NEED

6 x 4⅛-in. (15 x 10.5-cm) sheet of light green
   cardstock
Craft knife
Cutting mat
Ruler
Pencil
Decorative-edge scissors
8¼ x 6-in. (21 x 15-cm) sheet of dark green
   cardstock
Pricking tool
26-gauge (0.4 mm) silver wire
Wire cutters
Adhesive tape
Approximately 220 assorted green seed beads
Double-sided self-adhesive foam pads
2 x Spirella circles 2¼ in. (6 cm) and 2 in.
   (5 cm) in diameter
Dark green metallic embroidery thread

When a friend or work colleague moves on to pastures new, wish them all the best with this simple-to-make card. The combination of pretty embroidery thread and delicate beads are bound to make it a talking point at any going away party!

To make a matching gift tag, wrap a Spirella circle with embroidery thread, as in Step 5 of the card, then double mount it onto dark and then light green cardstock. Finally, make a hanger for the tag using a length of wire and about 40 seed beads.

1 Cut an 8¼ x 4⅛-in. (21 x 10.5-cm) piece of light green cardstock, and fold it in half to make the card blank. Using the decorative-edge scissors, cut a 4⅛-in. (10.5-cm) square of dark green cardstock.

2 On the dark green card, measure in ⅜ in. (1 cm) from each corner and make a small hole with a pricking tool. Cut a 30-in. (75-cm) length of 26-gauge (0.4 mm) silver wire and push one end through one of the holes. Bend it flat, and cover with adhesive tape to secure. Thread on 50–55 seed beads, so the beaded section reaches to the next hole.

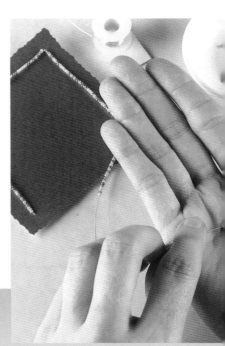

3 Thread the wire through the hole, run it along the back of the card, and bring it up to the front again through the next hole. Repeat the process for all four sides, securely fixing the end of the wire with adhesive tape.

4 Mount the beaded panel centrally on the folded card, using double-sided self-adhesive foam pads.

5 Now wrap the smaller Spirella circle with the metallic green embroidery thread, spacing the first wrap twelve spaces from the start of the wrap.

6 Using double-sided self-adhesive foam pads, mount the larger Spirella circle in the center of the beaded panel, with the smaller wrapped circle on top.

Mother's Day

Stamped, hand-colored butterflies make a pretty

Mother's Day card—and a few beads add sparkle and depth to the

design. If your mom's more interested in fashion than in flora and fauna,

you could embellish stamped images of shoes, handbags, or a glitzy designer

dress. Just follow the same method, highlighting details with beads.

YOU WILL NEED
Black dye ink pad
Rubber butterfly stamp
8¼ x 6-in. (21 x 15-cm) sheet of parchment paper
Water-soluble pencils
Water brush (or fine brush and pot of water)
Beading needle and thread
Approximately 30 orange seed beads
Wire coil maker
26-gauge (0.4 mm) orange wire
Wire cutters
8¼ x 6-in. (21 x 15-cm) yellow fun foam
22-gauge (0.6 mm) orange wire
Double-sided tape
4 orange eyelets
Eyelet setting tool
Bone folder
Card-folding board
12 x 8¼-in. (30 x 21-cm) sheet of orange cardstock
8¼ x 6-in. (21 x 15-cm) sheet of yellow cardstock
Decorative-edge scissors

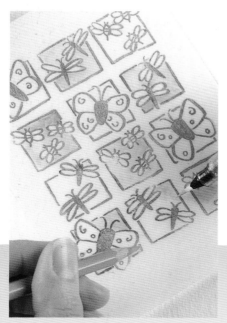

1 Using the black dye ink pad, stamp the image on the parchment paper and allow it to dry. When it is completely dry, color it in using water-soluble pencils.

2 Using a beading needle and thread, sew on seed beads to pick out elements of the design, such as the spots on the butterflies' wings.

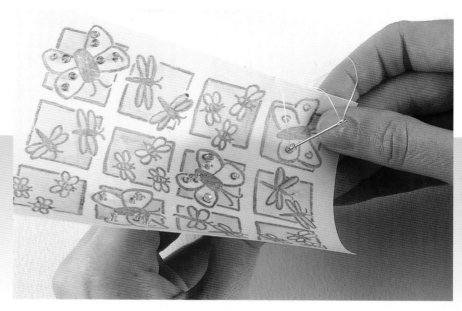

Make a matching gift tag using just part
of the stamped design.

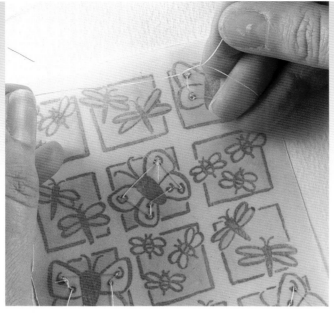

3 Carefully tie off the thread on the back of the parchment paper.

5 Pierce a hole in each corner of the foam. Cut two 12-in. (30-cm) lengths of 22-gauge (0.6 mm) orange wire, thread each one through a wire coil, and then thread the wires through the holes from the front.

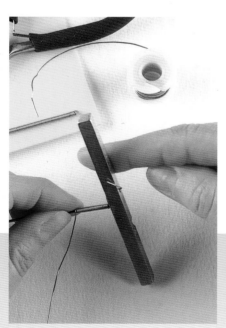

4 Cut a 5 x 7-in. (12.5 x 18-cm) piece of yellow fun foam. Using the wire coil maker, twist two coils of 26-gauge (0.4 mm) orange wire 4 in. (10 cm) long.

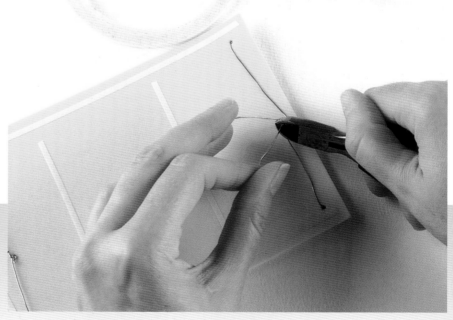

6 Place strips of double-sided tape around the outer edge and down the center of the foam. Twist the ends of wire together at the back of the fun foam to attach the coils firmly, and cut off any excess.

9 Using decorative-edge scissors, trim the yellow cardstock around all four edges. Center the yellow cardstock on the front of the card blank, with the fun foam on top. Using double-sided tape, stick the yellow card and foam to the left-hand flap of the card blank.

7 Center the stamped and colored parchment paper centrally on the fun foam and fix in place with an eyelet in each corner.

8 Using a bone folder and a card-folding board, fold the short sides of the orange cardstock in to the center of the piece to create a gatefold card.

You're a sport, Dad!

YOU WILL NEED

8¼ x 6-in. (21 x 15-cm) sheet of blue
  cardstock
Light green, mid-green, dark green, white, and
  yellow handmade papers
Spray adhesive
"Family" flexible push mold
Polymer clay (various colors)
2 black seed beads
Toothpick
Modeling tool
Hot glue gun

It's sometimes difficult to come up with good ideas for cards for men—but this delightful Father's Day card, based on Dad's favorite sport, is a definite winner. Even very young children can help to make this card. They'll love pushing clay into the mold to make the figure and tearing paper to create the landscape background.

It's easy to make other sporting or leisure scenes—such as soccer, basketball, or fishing—with simple polymer-clay models.

1 Fold the blue cardstock in half to make the card blank. Tear the handmade papers to create the landscape and stick them in place using spray adhesive.

2 Fill the mold for the male figure with the appropriate colors of polymer clay, making sure that the back is flat. Before you push the figure out of the mold, lightly score the back with a modeling tool, as this will help it adhere to the card in Step 5.

3 "Draw" a mouth using the tip of the toothpick, and add two black seed beads for the eyes. Roll out clay of the appropriate color to make the sporting props, and bake these and the male figure in the oven, following the manufacturer's instructions.

4 Attach the sporting props to the card using a hot glue gun.

5 Attach the male figure to the card using a hot glue gun. You will need to press the figure down firmly to ensure that it sticks.

Grandmother's day card

Show your grandmother just how special she is by sending this stamped and hand-colored card. There are lots of beautifully detailed botanical stamps on the market, and hand-coloring them creates the effect of an antique aquatint. A handmade envelope decorated with a section of the same motif is a lovely finishing touch.

YOU WILL NEED

Water brush (or fine brush and pot of water)

8¼ x 6-in. (21 x 15-cm) sheet of purple mulberry paper

12 x 8¼-in. (30 x 21-cm) sheet of light purple cardstock

8¼ x 6-in. (21 x 15-cm) sheet of dark purple cardstock

Craft knife

Cutting mat

Ruler

Pencil

Double-sided tape

Rubber botanical stamp

Black embossing powder

Clear embossing ink

Embossing ink pen

Heat gun

Water-soluble pencils

16½ x 12-in. (42 x 30-cm) sheet of watercolor paper

3 silver butterfly charms

28-gauge (0.3 mm) silver wire

Double-sided self-adhesive foam pads

FOR THE ENVELOPE

Template on page 153

To make the card

2 Cut an 11 x 7-in. (27.5 x 18-cm) piece of light purple cardstock and fold it in half to make the card blank. Cut a 4⅜ x 5⅛-in. (11 x 13-cm) piece of dark purple cardstock. Using double-sided tape, layer first the mulberry paper and then the dark purple cardstock centrally onto the card blank.

1 Tear a 4¾ x 5½-in. (12 x 14-cm) piece of mulberry paper. (To make it easier to tear, brush the area you want to tear with water, to soften the paper fibers.)

HYDRANGEA
Hydrangeaceae

GRANDMOTHER'S DAY CARD

3 Using clear embossing ink, stamp the botanical image on a small piece of watercolor paper. Sprinkle on black embossing powder and heat with a heat gun until the powder fuses.

4 Using the water-soluble pencils and water brush, color in the stamped image.

To make a matching gift tag, take just part of the stamped design, cut it out, and attach it to a small piece of card.

To make the envelope

5 Tear the watercolor paper to slightly smaller than the dark purple cardstock. Cut short lengths of 28-gauge (0.3 mm) wire, and thread them through the loops at the top of the butterfly charms. Make a small hole in the stamped image, push through the wire, and secure on the reverse. Center the stamped image on the purple cardstock and fix in place using self-adhesive foam pads.

1 Transfer the template on page 153 onto the remaining watercolor paper, and score and fold along the crease lines. Using the embossing pen, ink over just a small section of the botanical stamp. Stamp the image in the bottom left-hand corner of the envelope, then heat emboss and color, as in Steps 3 and 4 of the main card.

2 Using double-sided tape, make up the envelope.

For the best Granddad in the world

YOU WILL NEED

12 x 8¼-in. (30 x 21-cm) sheet of cream cardstock

Craft knife

Cutting mat

Ruler

Pencil

8¼ x 6-in. (21 x 15-cm) sheet of light brown
    mulberry paper

Water brush (or fine brush and pot of water)

Eraser

8¼ x 6-in. (21 x 15-cm) sheet of copper-colored
    cardstock

Spray glue

4 mini eyelets

Punch and eyelet setter

24 in. (60 cm) decorative thread

Photocopy of map

Glue stick

Rubber car stamp

Black pigment ink

Black embossing powder

Heat gun

Scissors

Double-sided self-adhesive foam pads

This card is so versatile it can be used to tell your Granddad you love him, wish him a happy birthday or simply to say "thank you." By weaving a map that features a place in the world that is dear to his heart, you can rekindle fond memories of a honeymoon or a favorite vacation destination.

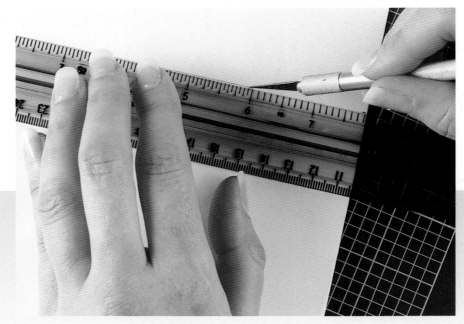

1   Fold the cream cardstock in half, short edge to short edge. Cut the folded card blank to 6 in. (15 cm) square.

2 Mark out a 5-in. (12.5-cm) square of mulberry paper. Use the water brush or fine brush and water to "draw" around the section you have marked out.

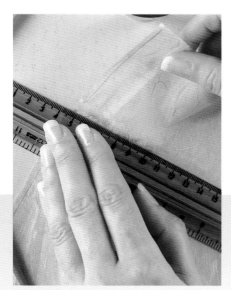

3 Tear along the damp line, using the ruler to ensure a straight line. Let the edge of the mulberry paper dry, then carefully erase the pencil marks.

4 Measure a 4-in. (10-cm) square of copper-colored cardstock, then tear along the edge using the ruler to ensure a straight line.

5 Using the spray adhesive, mount the mulberry paper and the copper cardstock centrally on the front card blank. Using the punch and eyelet setter, fix the four eyelets into position.

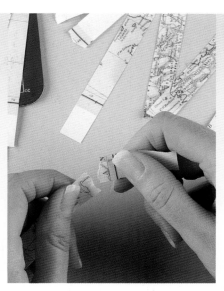

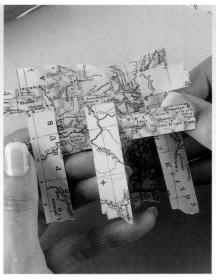

6 Thread the decorative thread through the eyelets and knot at the top, at the front of the greeting card.

7 From the map cut nine strips ⅝ in. (1.5 m) wide and at least 4 ½ in. (12 cm) long. Tear the ends off each strip, so they are about 4 in. (10 cm) long.

8 Weave the strips together to create the background. To hold them in place as you weave, dab a small amount of dry glue stick on the ends of each strip. Once woven, mount centrally on the card blank with spray adhesive.

9 Stamp the car on the piece of cream cardstock left over from Step 1. Sprinkle embossing powder over the stamped image and heat with a heat gun until the powder fuses. Carefully cut out the car image and mount it on the card blank with double-sided self-adhesive foam pads.

Christmas angel

We've used a delightful little angel stamp for this card, but there are so many lovely rubber stamps on the market that you could easily adapt the design to suit another motif. The beauty of tearing the layers of paper is that you don't have to worry about exact measurements or making sure your cuts are absolutely square, which really speeds up the card-making process – and it looks great, too.

YOU WILL NEED

Rubber angel stamp

Waterproof black dye ink pad

8¼ x 6-in. (21 x 15-cm) sheet of watercolor paper

Water-soluble pencils

Water brush (or fine brush and pot of water)

12 x 8¼-in. (30 x 21-in) sheet of pearlescent ivory cardstock

8¼ x 6-in. (21 x 15-cm) sheet of pearlescent green cardstock

8¼ x 6-in. (21 x 15-cm) sheet of handmade paper

Glitter glue

Double-sided self-adhesive foam pads

Double-sided tape

1 Using a black, waterproof ink pad, stamp the angel onto the watercolor paper.

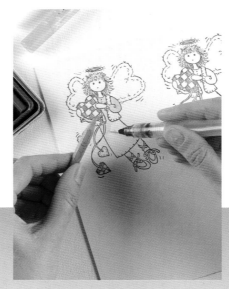

2 Using water-soluble pencils and a water brush, color in the image, picking up the color from the pencil tip on the tip of the brush. Leave to dry.

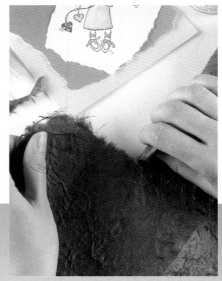

3 Fold the pearlescent ivory cardstock in half to make the card blank. Tear around the edges of the green cardstock, the handmade paper, and the stamped watercolor paper, making each layer slightly smaller than the previous one.

Change the colors, papers, and number of layers used to make slightly different versions of this card for all your family and friends.

4 Highlight some of the stamped design with glitter glue and leave to dry. Using double-sided tape for the first two layers, and self-adhesive foam pads for the last layer, assemble all the pieces of card, placing the stamped angel design centrally.

CHRISTMAS ANGEL

Happy New Year!

YOU WILL NEED

Templates on page 154–155
Pencil
Ruler
Cutting mat
Craft knife
8¼ x 6-in. (21 x 15-cm) sheet of light green cardstock
8¼ x 6-in. (21 x 15-cm) sheet of metallic green cardstock
Double-sided tape
26-gauge (0.4 mm) silver wire
Wire cutters
Approximately 100 assorted green seed beads
Round-nose pliers
Hot glue gun
Two wooden chopsticks
Double-sided self-adhesive foam pads
Two 12 x 8¼-in. (30 x 21-cm) sheets of green cardstock
2 x 6-in. (5 x 15-cm) strip of silver cardstock
Paper crimper/ribbler
Approximately 15 flat-backed gemstones
Craft glue
Embossing tool

Usher in the New Year with a bang with this colorful pop-up firework card. Although it looks a little complicated, it's really very easy to make—and the sparkly beads and gemstones bring the design to life. What's more, no one will guess you used a chopstick in the design!

For a simpler version of this greeting card, decorate just the outside and omit the pop-up inside.

1 Using the templates from page 155, cut two rocket base shapes from light green cardstock and two highlight shapes from metallic green cardstock.

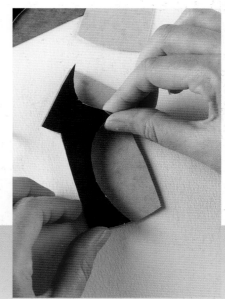

2 Using double-sided tape, attach one highlight shape to each rocket.

3 Cut two 10-in. (25-cm) and two 8-in. (20-cm) lengths of 26-gauge
(0.4 mm) silver wire. Fold each one in half and twist the first ⅜ in.
(1 cm) or so. Thread a few beads onto one side of the wire, then make
a loop by twisting the wire around the shaft of your round-nose pliers.
Repeat the process along the length of the wire, and with the remaining
pieces of wire.

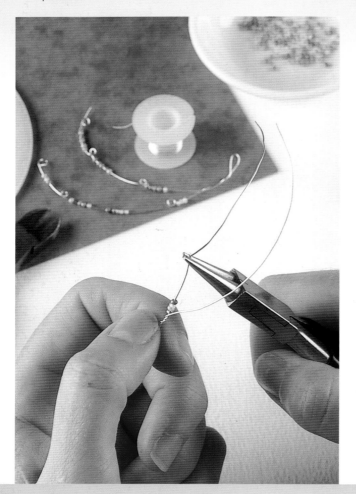

4 Using a hot glue gun, attach the longer strands to the back of the first
rocket (this will be for the outside of the card), and the shorter ones to
the back of the second rocket.

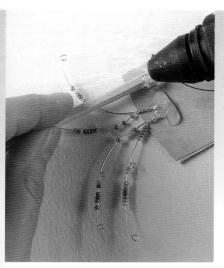

5 Cut 3 in. (7.5 cm) off the end of each chopstick and attach one to the back of each rocket, gluing the cut end to hide it.

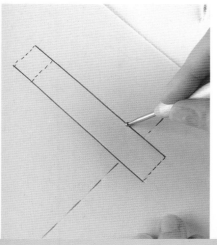

6 Fold one piece of green cardstock in half to make the card blank. Run the silver card through the paper crimper/ribbler, center it on the front of the card, and stick in place using self-adhesive foam pads. Using double-sided self-adhesive foam pads, attach the rocket with the longer wire sections to the center of the ribbled card. Stick a few flat-backed gemstones onto the green card, positioning them randomly.

7 Copy the template on page 154. Using an embossing tool, transfer the fold and cut lines onto the back of the second piece of green card to make the insert card.

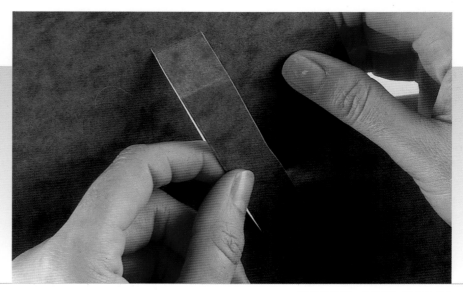

8 Trim ⅛ in. (3 mm) from one long and one short side of the insert card. Cut the tab, then fold the card and pull out the tab.

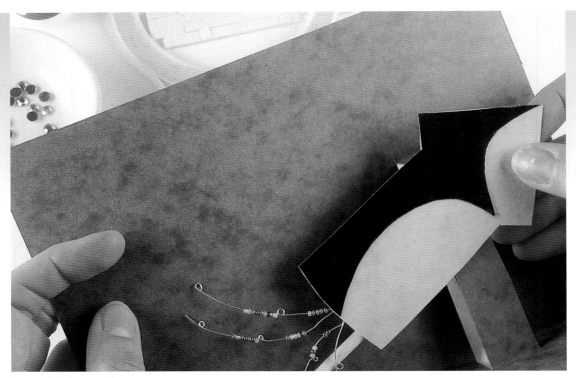

9 Using double-sided tape, attach the rocket to the tab at an angle

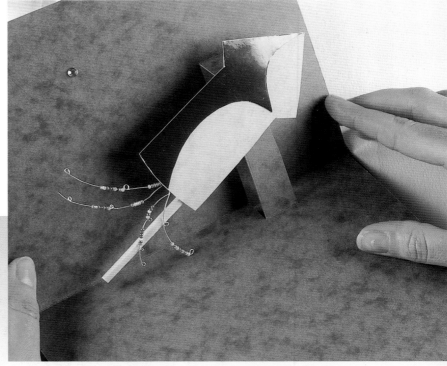

10 Randomly stick a few gemstones over the insert card. Apply double-sided tape to the back of the insert, then stick it inside the main card.

Be my Valentine!

For that special person in your life, here's an elegant, sophisticated-looking Valentine card that will set their heart racing—and there's an extra surprise on the inside. It's so elegant that you'll want to spoil the guessing game by signing it!

YOU WILL NEED

- 12 x 8¼-in. (30 x 21-cm) sheet of light pink cardstock
- Craft knife
- Cutting mat
- Ruler
- Pencil
- Template on page 156
- Two 12 x 8¼-in. (30 x 21-cm) sheets of heart decorated paper
- 12 x 8¼-in. (30 x 21-cm) sheet of dark pink cardstock
- Double-sided tape
- 8¼ x 6-in. (21 x 15-cm) sheet of red cardstock
- Decorative-edge scissors
- 1-in. (4-cm)-wide gold ribbon
- Pink and red polymer clay
- 12 x 8¼-in. (30 x 21-cm) tracing paper
- Rolling pin (or pasta machine)
- Large heart-shaped cookie cutter
- Baking tray
- Hot glue gun

1 Trim ⅛ in. (3 mm) from one short and one long side of the light pink cardstock. Fold it in half. Using the template on page 156, draw half a heart shape along the folded edge and cut out.

2 Fold the two side edges back to the center fold, creasing sharply.

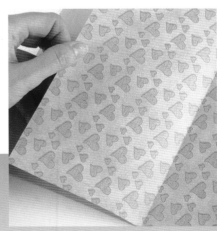

3 Trim 2 in. (5 cm) from one short edge of one piece of heart-decorated paper, and fold it in half. Fold the dark pink cardstock in half to make the card blank. Apply double-sided tape along the two short edges of the heart-decorated paper, and insert it into the card blank.

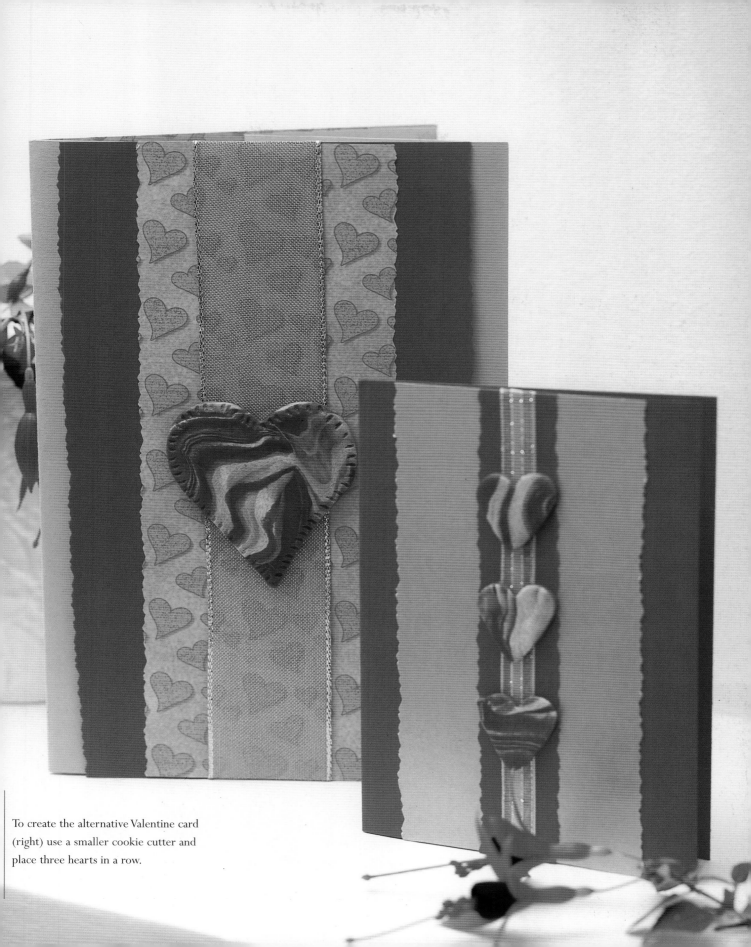

To create the alternative Valentine card
(right) use a smaller cookie cutter and
place three hearts in a row.

top tip

■ *If you can't find a*
ready-made paper
that's suitable,
decorate a sheet of
white or cream
handmade paper by
stamping tiny red
hearts all over it.

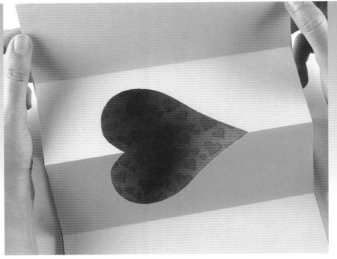

4 Apply double-sided tape to the outside, top, and bottom edges of the outer flaps of the cut-out card, and attach to the inside of the card blank, so that the decorated paper can be seen through the aperture.

5 Using decorative-edge scissors, cut around all four edges of the red cardstock.

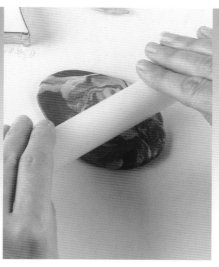

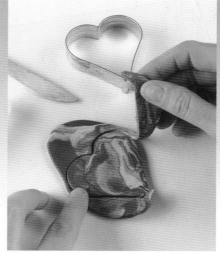

6 Cut a strip 3 in. (7.5 cm) wide from the second piece of heart-decorated paper. Using double-sided tape, center the hearts paper on the red cardstock with the gold ribbon on top, wrapping the ends of the ribbon around the back for neatness.

7 Take one-third of each block of polymer clay and roll it into a sausage shape. Wrap one color of clay around the other, form into a ball, place on the tracing paper, and roll out to about ⅛ in. (3 mm) thick. The two colors will merge together, creating a marbled effect.

8 Press a heart-shaped cookie cutter into the clay to cut out the shape.

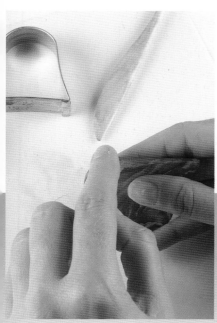

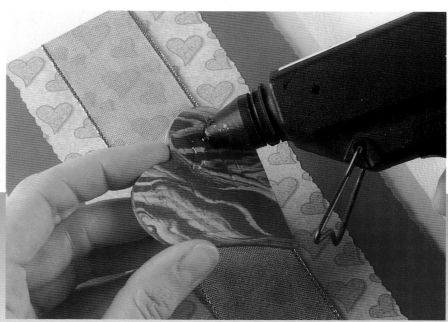

9 Neaten the edges of the clay heart with your fingertips. Place the heart on a baking tray and bake following the manufacturer's instructions.

10 Leave the polymer clay heart to cool, then attach to the front of the card using a hot glue gun.

Place cards

Extra little touches such as place setting cards can really make a party—so why not have a go at our simple-to-make projects? They're guaranteed to provide a talking point—and they're so lovely that your guests are sure to want to take them home as souvenirs of the event. We've used a wide variety of techniques from stamping to collage, and materials ranging from buttons to leaves, so you are guaranteed to be provided with year-round inspiration.

Wedding reception

For a large-scale event such as a wedding reception, you need a place-setting card that can be made quickly in large quantities, but still looks stylish. This one fits the bill perfectly.

YOU WILL NEED

⅜-in. (1-cm) red quilling paper

Craft glue

Toothpick

Quilling tool

⅜-in. (1-cm) green quilling paper

Quilling design board

12 x 8¼-in. (30 x 21-cm) sheet of red cardstock

White handmade paper

Craft knife

Cutting mat

Ruler

Double-sided tape

Silver peel 'n' stick borders

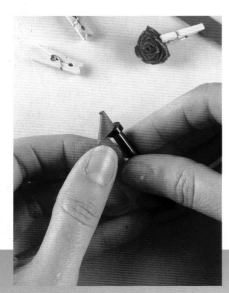

1 Place the end of a strip ⅜-in. (1-cm) red quilling paper into the quilling tool and turn it twice. Now fold the paper away and down from you to create a crease across the paper at 45 degrees.

2 Twirl the tool, keeping the edge of the paper at the base of the tool; this will make the paper flare out. When you reach the end of the creased section, fold it again at 45 degrees and repeat the process. Continue until you reach the end of the paper strip, then glue the end in place.

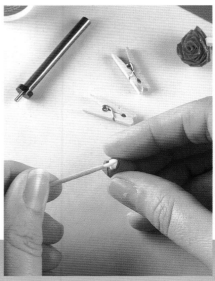

3 Remove the rose from the quilling tool, dab a little craft glue on the back of the rose with the toothpick, and hold in place with a small craft peg until the glue has dried completely.

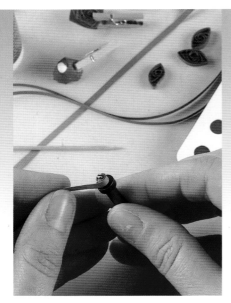

top tips

■ To prevent the cards from popping open while you are decorating the front, use a couple of small craft pegs (such as the wooden ones used here) to hold them in place.

■ If the end of the quilling paper keeps coming out of the quilling tool, dampen the end of the paper slightly before you insert it.

4 To make the leaves, insert a strip of green quilling paper into the quilling tool and twirl it until you reach the end of the strip. Drop the quilled leaf into the design board and allow the coil to "relax."

5 Glue the end in place, then pinch the ends between your thumbs and index fingers to form the leaf shape. Make one rose and two or three leaves for each card.

6 Cut a 4-in. (10-cm) square of red cardstock and fold it in half. Cut a 3½ x 1½-in. (9 x 4-cm) rectangle of white handmade paper and attach it centrally to the folded red card blank, using double-sided tape.

7 Outline the white handmade paper with silver peel 'n' stick borders.

8 Apply a little craft glue to the back of each leaf with the toothpick and stick them in place. Apply glue to the back of the rose in the same way and stick it in the center, between the leaves.

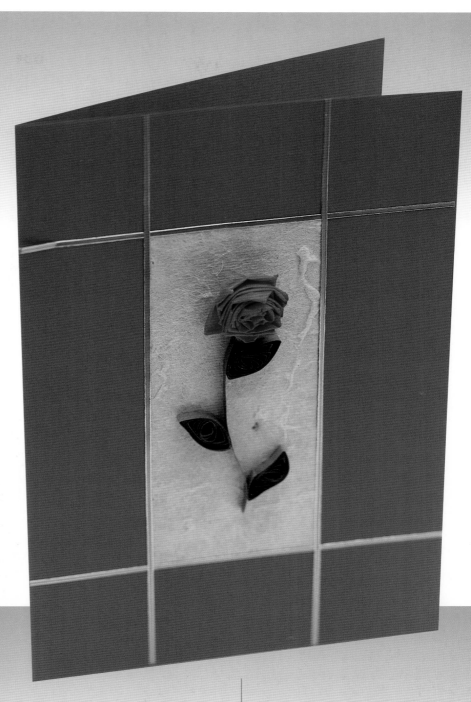

For a thoroughly coordinated look, make matching invitations and thank you cards.

Beware the witching hour...

A pop-up Jack-'o-lantern card is perfect for a Halloween party, when spooks and specters come out to play and all kinds of devilish mischief is afoot. Who know whose eyes will be watching the ghostly goings-on..!

YOU WILL NEED

12 x 8¼-in. (30 x 21-cm) sheet of black cardstock

Craft knife

Cutting mat

Ruler

Googly eyes

Craft glue

Silver gel pen

Paper crimper/ribbler

8¼ x 6-in. (21 x 15-cm) sheet of orange cardstock

Template on page 156

Fine black marker pen

Double-sided tape

1 Cut a 3 x 6-in. (7.5 x 15-cm) piece of black cardstock and fold it in half to make the card blank. With the fold at the bottom, attach pairs of googly eyes, then draw in the eyebrows with a silver gel pen keeping the back of the folded card on the table.

2 Cut a 2 ⅜ x 5 ⅛-in. (6 x 13-cm) piece of black cardstock. Run it through the paper crimper/ribbler, and fold it in half. In the center of the folded edge, cut a tab ⅜ in. (1 cm) wide and ⅜ in. (1 cm) deep. Push the tab to the inside of the card.

3 Transfer the pumpkin template on page 156 onto orange cardstock. Cut it out and draw in the details using a black marker pen.

■ *To transfer a template onto card, photocopy the template to the size required, place the card under the photocopy, and emboss using an embossing tool as shown in Step 3. You can then follow the indents on the card without having to worry about erasing any unwanted pencil lines.*

To make the speedy alternative shown above left, cut a 4-in. (10-cm) square of orange cardstock and a 3½ x 1½-in. (9 x 4-cm) piece of black cardstock. Fold the orange cardstock in half, center the black cardstock on the front using double-sided foam pads, and attach a pumpkin motif to the right-hand side. For an even quicker card, stick a couple of googly eyes onto the black cardstock and draw in some eyebrows.

4 Using double-sided tape, attach the ribbled card to the inside of the card blank, making sure that the tab pops out. Using double-sided tape, attach the pumpkin to the tab so that it pops up when the card is opened. (The person sitting opposite will see the googly eyes added in Step 1.)

Christmas cheer

YOU WILL NEED

12 x 8¼-in. (30 x 21-cm) sheet of gold
    cardstock

Craft knife

Cutting mat

Ruler

Parchment paper

Double-sided tape

Rubber snowman stamp

Clear embossing ink

12 x 8¼-in. (30 x 21-cm) sheet of cream
    cardstock

Black embossing powder

Heat gun

Water-soluble pencils

Water brush (or fine brush and pot of water)

Scissors

12 x 8¼-in. (30 x 21-cm) sheet of red cardstock

Double-sided self-adhesive foam pads

If you are in a hurry and want a quicker alternative, fold the red card in half, layer it with parchment paper, and attach a single stamped image.

Christmas is a time of celebration, to be shared with family and friends. Bring extra cheer to your table with these jolly 3-D snowmen place settings. To make it a real family occasion, get the children to help color in the snowmen motifs with water-soluble pencils.

1   Cut a 4 x 2-in. (10 x 5-cm) piece of gold cardstock. Tear a 3½ x 3-in. (9 x 7.5-cm) piece of parchment paper.

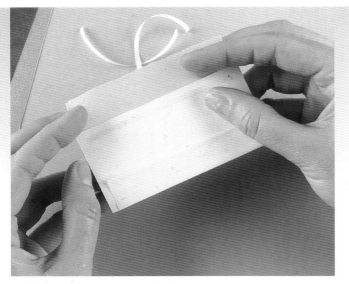

2 Wrap the parchment paper around the gold card, and fix it in place on the reverse with double-sided tape.

3 Using clear embossing ink, stamp the image four times on cream card. (You need three, but it's a good idea to stamp an extra motif to allow for any mistakes made when cutting out the parts.) Sprinkle on the black embossing powder.

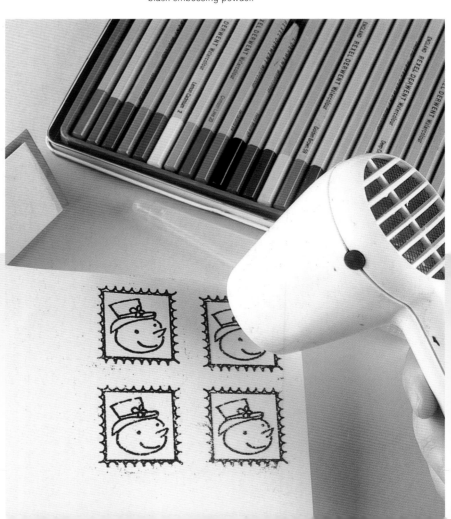

4 Tip off the excess embossing powder then heat with a heat gun until the powder melts and fuses.

top tip

- *If you do not have parchment paper, use tracing paper instead.*

PLACE CARDS

5 Color in the image using water-soluble pencils and the water brush or fine brush and pot of water.

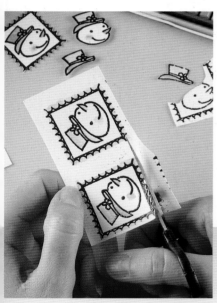

6 Cut out the whole image from one stamped motif, just the face from the second motif, and just the hat from the third.

7 Cut a 4¼-in. (11-cm) square of red cardstock and fold it in half to make the card blank. Using double-sided tape, stick the gold-and-parchment panel on top. Use double-sided self-adhesive foam pads to layer the three sections of the stamped image to create a 3-D effect, then attach it to the right-hand side of the card with more double-sided self-adhesive foam pads.

Spring surprise

A quilled flower in fresh, spring colors is the focal point
of this place-setting card. It would make a lovely addition to the
breakfast table when you have house guests—and it's ideal for an Easter
brunch or lunch.

YOU WILL NEED

12 x 8¼-in. (30 x 21-cm) sheet of orange
  cardstock
Cutting mat
Craft knife
Ruler
Pencil
12 x 8¼-in. (30 x 21-cm) sheet of parchment
  paper
⅛ in. (3 mm) orange quilling paper
⅛ in. (3 mm) pale green quilling paper
⅛ in. (3 mm) yellow quilling paper
Quilling tool
Quilling design board
Clear-drying craft glue
Toothpick
Double-sided tape

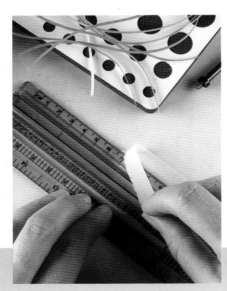

1 Tear a 4-in. (10-cm) square of parchment
paper for use in Step 3.

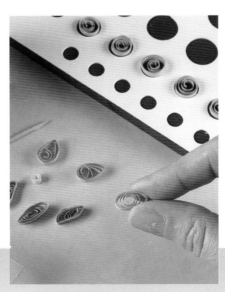

2 Quill the following: eight loose orange
circles, three loose green circles, and one
tight yellow coil. Pinch one end of the
orange circles to form teardrop shapes and
both ends of the green circles to form neat
leaf shapes.

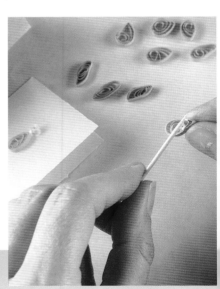

3 Fold the parchment paper in half. Using
craft glue, attach the yellow coil to the
right-hand corner, about 1 in. (2.5 cm) up
and 1 in. (2.5 cm) in from the edge. Now
attach the orange teardrop shapes around
the yellow coil by placing a little craft glue
along one edge with the toothpick. Attach
the green leaves using the same technique.

Use the same method to create invitations to a spring party. This simple card (left) was made using four eyelets, some parchment paper, and matching decorative cord.

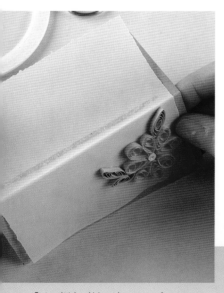

4 Cut a 4¼-in. (11-cm) square of orange cardstock and fold it in half to make the card blank. Apply double-sided tape along the top back edge, just below the fold, and place the parchment around the card to complete the place setting.

Summer splendor

One of the joys of papercrafting is that you can borrow from so many other crafts, including weaving. The technique is used to great effect on these place settings for a summer lunch whether indoors or in the garden. Zingy shades of sunshine yellow and a pretty little sun-hat charm give the design a bright summery feel.

YOU WILL NEED

12 x 8¼-in. (30 x 21-cm) sheet of lilac cardstock
Craft knife
Cutting mat
Ruler
Pencil
Narrow double-sided tape
⅛ in. (3 mm) bright yellow quilling paper
⅛ in. (3 mm) pale yellow quilling paper
Craft glue
Charms
Double-sided tape

1 Cut a 5-in. (12.5-cm) square of lilac cardstock, score down the center of the wrong side and fold it in half.

2 Apply double-sided tape down the right-hand side of the card. Attach strips of quilling paper horizontally, alternating shades of yellow and increasing the length of the strips, as shown. The top piece should be about 1¼ in. (3 cm) long and the bottom piece about 3 in. (7.5 cm).

3 Weave lengths of quilling paper vertically in and out of the horizontal strips, alternating the shades of yellow and securing each piece as you go with tiny dabs of craft glue.

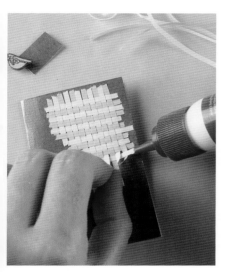

4 Glue the ends firmly in place so that they cannot unravel.

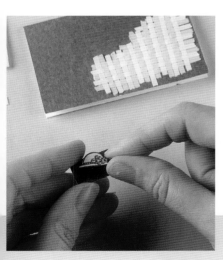

5 Using a double-sided self-adhesive foam pad, attach a charm to a small piece of card. Mount the charm in the center of the weaving, using double-sided tape.

For truly individual place settings, use a different charm for each guest.

top tip

■ *If your bottle of craft glue does not have a fine nozzle, apply the glue using a toothpick.*

Tea time in the fall

For classy-looking autumnal place settings, dyed skeleton leaves look absolutely stunning. Use warm colors—burgundy and orange—to echo the natural colors of the season.

YOU WILL NEED

12 x 8¼-in. (30 x 21-cm) sheet of burgundy cardstock
Craft knife
Cutting mat
Ruler
Pencil
12 x 8¼-in. (30 x 21-cm) sheet of cream cardstock
Skeleton leaves in two colors
Spray adhesive
Scissors
Double-sided self-adhesive foam pads

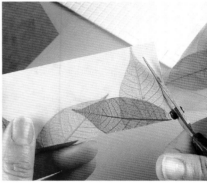

3 Along the bottom and right-hand edges, cut away the cardstock following the shape of the leaves. If necessary, trim a little along the top edge.

1 Cut a 4¼-in. (11-cm) square of burgundy cardstock, fold it in half to make the card blank, and set aside. Cut a 4 x 2-in. (10 x 5-cm) piece of cream cardstock. Using spray adhesive, glue skeleton leaves along the right and bottom edges, alternating the colors and overlapping them slightly.

2 Cut off any sections of leaves that overhang the edge of the card. (You can use them to make other place settings.)

4 Using double-sided self-adhesive foam pads, mount the decorated cream card centrally on the front of the card blank.

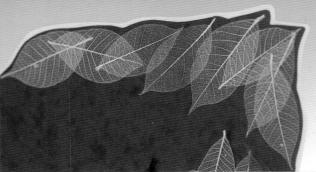

To make matching invitations, cut two pieces of cardstock, the first measuring 8 x 4 in. (20 x 10 cm) and the second 7½ x 3½ in. (19 x 9 cm). Attach overlapping leaves to the smaller of the two pieces along one long and one short edge. On the outer edges only, cut around the leaf shapes. Mount the decorated panel on the larger card, then cut this card, too, to follow the shapes of the leaves as shown, left.

Winter warmth

Banish the chill of winter by inviting friends to a

warming supper—and perhaps a glass or two of mulled wine. Making

these place-setting cards is a great way to use up scraps of mulberry or

handmade paper left over from other projects. Embossing a motif on the

front of the card—in this case, a simple outline leaf shape—is a subtle but

sophisticated finishing touch.

YOU WILL NEED
12 x 8¼-in. (30 x 21-cm) sheet of cream cardstock
Craft knife
Cutting mat
Ruler
Yellow and orange mulberry paper
Spray adhesive
Scissors
Decorative-edge scissors
Template on page 156
Pencil
Light box
Embossing tool
Double-sided self-adhesive foam pads

1 Cut a 5-in. (12.5-cm) square of cream cardstock, and fold it in half to make the card blank. Tear the mulberry paper into small rectangles.

2 Using spray adhesive, stick the mulberry paper onto the card blank, alternating the colors and covering it completely. Turn the card over and cut off any mulberry paper that overhangs the edges.

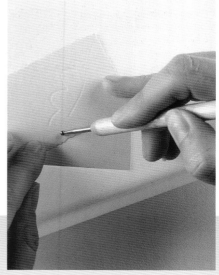

3 Using decorative-edge scissors, cut a 2 x 4-in. (5 x 10-cm) piece of cream cardstock. Using the template on page 156, make a stencil. Place the stencil on a light box, with one corner of the card on top. Using an embossing tool, draw around the outline of the motif.

Create a matching invitation or thank you card using the same method, but emboss several overlapping leaves.

4 Using double-sided self-adhesive foam pads, mount the embossed panel centrally on the front of the card blank.

Party playtime

Looking for a kids' party activity with a difference?

Then let the little ones make their own place-setting cards. This design uses a cute teddy bear design stamped onto shrink plastic. Make all the card blanks and stamp the motifs in advance, then let the children color them in. They'll be fascinated to see how much the plastic shrinks when you heat it—but do make sure that curious little hands are kept well away from the heat gun and any sharp craft tools.

YOU WILL NEED

12 x 8¼-in. (30 x 21-cm) sheet of pink cardstock

Cutting mat

Craft knife

Ruler

Pencil

Rubber stamp

Black dye ink pad

Clear shrink plastic

Sandpaper (if surface of shrink plastic has not been sanded)

Coloring pencils

Scissors

Hole punch

12 x 8¼-in. (30 x 21-cm) sheet of parchment paper

Pricking tool

Heat gun

Paper fasteners

1 Cut the pink cardstock in half widthwise. (You can get two place settings from each 12 x 8¼-in. (30 x 21-cm) sheet of cardstock.) Fold it in half, then fold the top section back in half again. If necessary, lightly sand the shrink plastic.

2 Stamp the image onto the shrink plastic and allow it to dry completely.

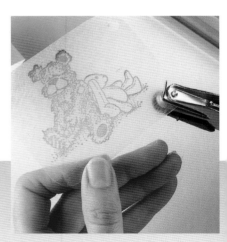

3 Cut out the design, then punch a hole in each corner.

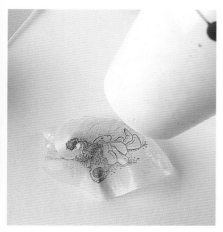

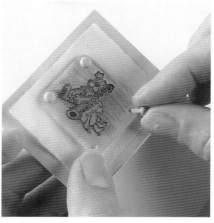

4 Get the children to color in their own picture. Heat the plastic with the heat gun yourself, and allow it to cool before allowing anyone to handle it.

Most card makers rapidly build up a large stock of rubber stamps—so try out this project using different stamps from your collection.

5 Tear the parchment paper so that it is slightly larger than the shrunk plastic image. Place the parchment paper on the smaller section of the folded card. Place the shrink plastic centrally over this then prick the holes through the shrink plastic.

6 Attach the shrunk design and parchment paper to the card blank using paper fasteners.

top tips

- *To find out whether the shrink plastic needs to be sanded, run your fingertips over it. If it feels smooth to the touch, then it needs to be lightly sanded; if it feels slightly rough, it does not.*
- *When choosing which stamp to use, do a test run first to see what size it shrinks to and adjust the size of the card to fit if necessary.*
- *When coloring a design stamped on shrink plastic, make sure that the colors are not too dark. As the plastic shrinks, the colors darken—so if you start off with very dark colors, the stamped outline will merge into the rest of the design.*
- *Press the reverse of the stamp firmly onto the shrink plastic while it is still warm, to get it to lie flat.*

Button place setting

If you are planning a party with lots of youngsters, you may have very little time to make place settings. Solve the problem with these button cards, which are quick and easy to make.

2 Cut a 1½-in. (4-cm) square of fabric and fray the edges.

3 Using spray adhesive, attach the fabric centrally to the smaller section of the folded card blank.

YOU WILL NEED

12 x 8¼-in. (30 x 21-cm) cream cardstock
Cutting mat
Craft knife
Ruler
Pencil
Evenweave cotton fabric
Scissors
Spray adhesive
Craft glue
Decorative ceramic button

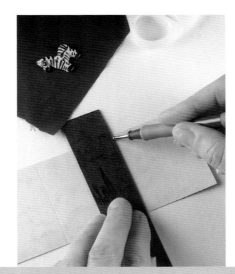

1 Cut the cardstock in half widthwise. (You can get two place settings from each 12 x 8¼-in. (30 x 21-cm) sheet of cardstock.) Fold it in half, then fold the top section back in half again to make the card blank.

top tip

■ *If the glue comes through the holes of your button, use double-sided self-adhesive foam pads instead.*

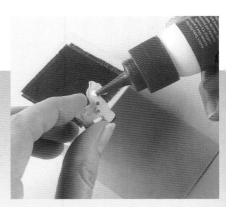

4 Using craft glue, attach a ceramic button centrally to the frayed fabric.

Templates

This chapter contains all the template designs used in the book. Page numbers refer you to the places where the motifs are used. To use, photocopy the templates (enlarging where necessary) and trace around them. Except where indicated, all the motifs are shown actual size. To make the stencils on pages 147, 151, and 156, photocopy your chosen design then transfer it onto thin cardstock. Do this by tracing over the photocopied line with a soft pencil, then rub the back of the photocopy with a pencil to transfer the design. Carefully cut out the stencil using a craft knife on a cutting mat.

VROOM, VROOM!
PAGE 21

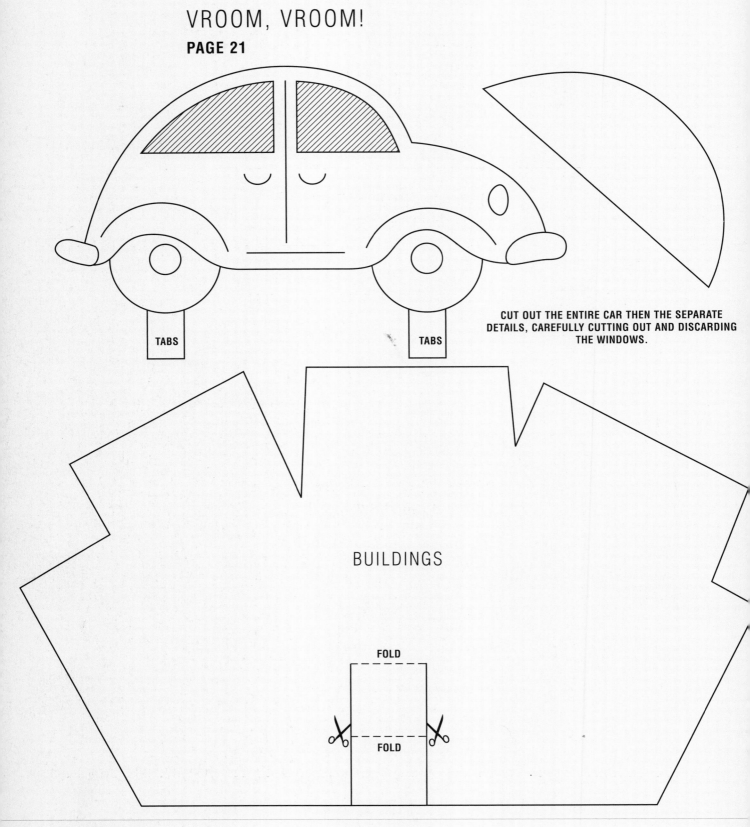

CUT OUT THE ENTIRE CAR THEN THE SEPARATE
DETAILS, CAREFULLY CUTTING OUT AND DISCARDING
THE WINDOWS.

TABS

TABS

BUILDINGS

FOLD

FOLD

CENTRAL LINE

ROAD ON FRONT OF CARD
(ENLARGE BY 10%)

ROAD INSIDE THE CARD
(ENLARGE BY 10%)

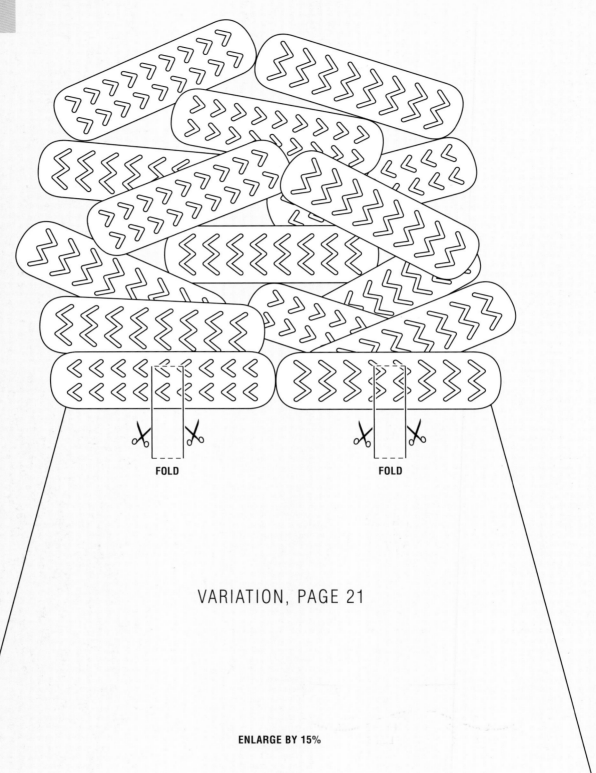

FOLD

FOLD

VARIATION, PAGE 21

ENLARGE BY 15%

JUMBO IN THE JUNGLE
PAGE 24

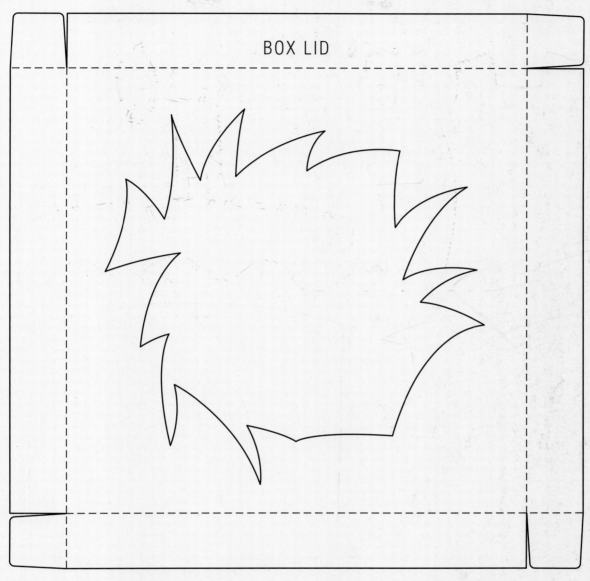

BOX LID

TO MAKE THE BOX BASE, CUT OUT THE LID
SHAPE BUT NOT THE APERTURE. MAKE THE BOX
BASE A FRACTION SMALLER SO THE LID FITS
OVER IT EASILY.

STENCIL

YOU'RE A STAR!
PAGE 33

SWEET SIXTEEN
PAGE 36

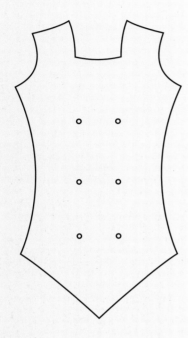

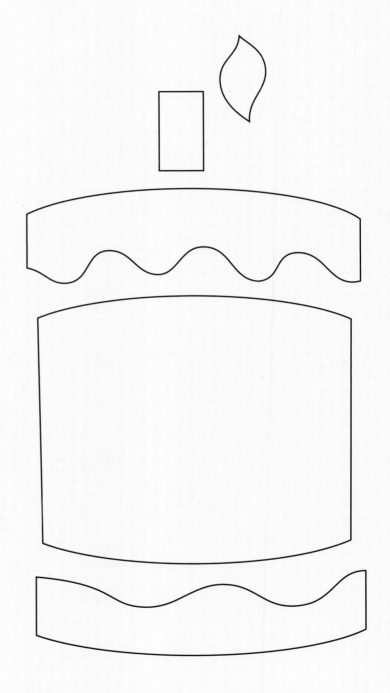

POP!
PAGE 40

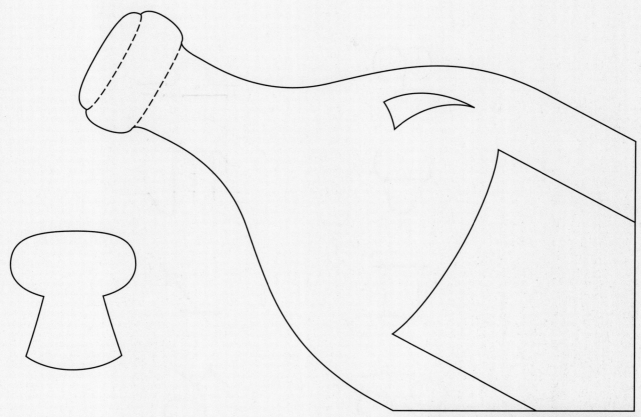

CUT OUT THE CORK AND THE ENTIRE BOTTLE
TEMPLATES ONCE. MAKE A SEPARATE TEMPLATE
FOR THE LABEL ON THE BOTTLE.

ZODIAC BIRTHDAY
PAGE 58

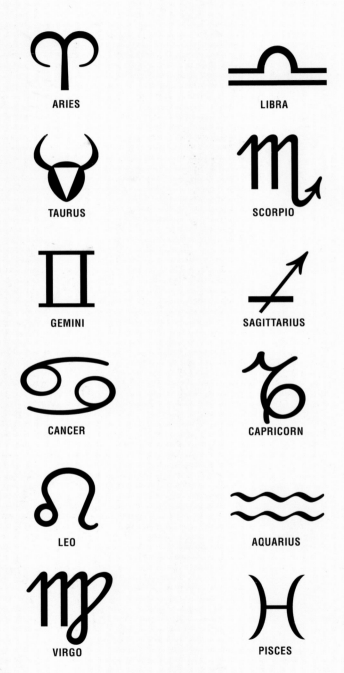

ARIES

TAURUS

GEMINI

CANCER

LEO

VIRGO

LIBRA

SCORPIO

SAGITTARIUS

CAPRICORN

AQUARIUS

PISCES

IN SYMPATHY
PAGE 80

STENCIL

PASSED WITH FLYING
COLORS!
PAGE 76

WELCOME TO YOUR
NEW HOME
PAGE 80

CUT OUT THE FRONT, ROOF, AND CHIMNEY OF THE
HOUSE TWICE, CAREFULLY CUTTING OUT AND
DISCARDING THE WINDOWS. CUT OUT EIGHT
SETS OF CURTAINS.

GRANDMOTHER'S DAY

PAGE 98

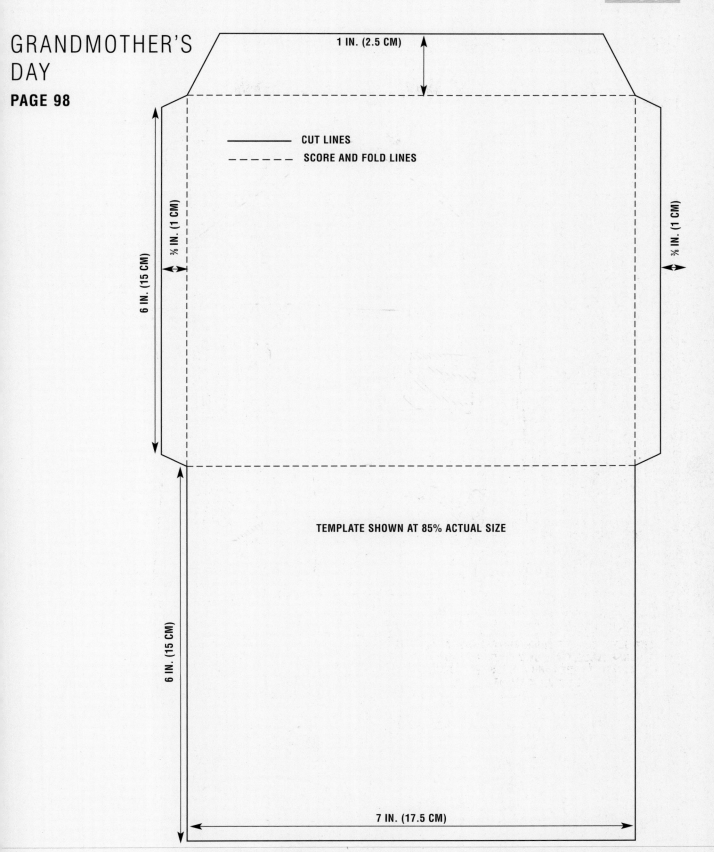

1 IN. (2.5 CM)

CUT LINES

SCORE AND FOLD LINES

⅜ IN. (1 CM)

6 IN. (15 CM)

⅜ IN. (1 CM)

TEMPLATE SHOWN AT 85% ACTUAL SIZE

6 IN. (15 CM)

7 IN. (17.5 CM)

HAPPY NEW YEAR

PAGE 109

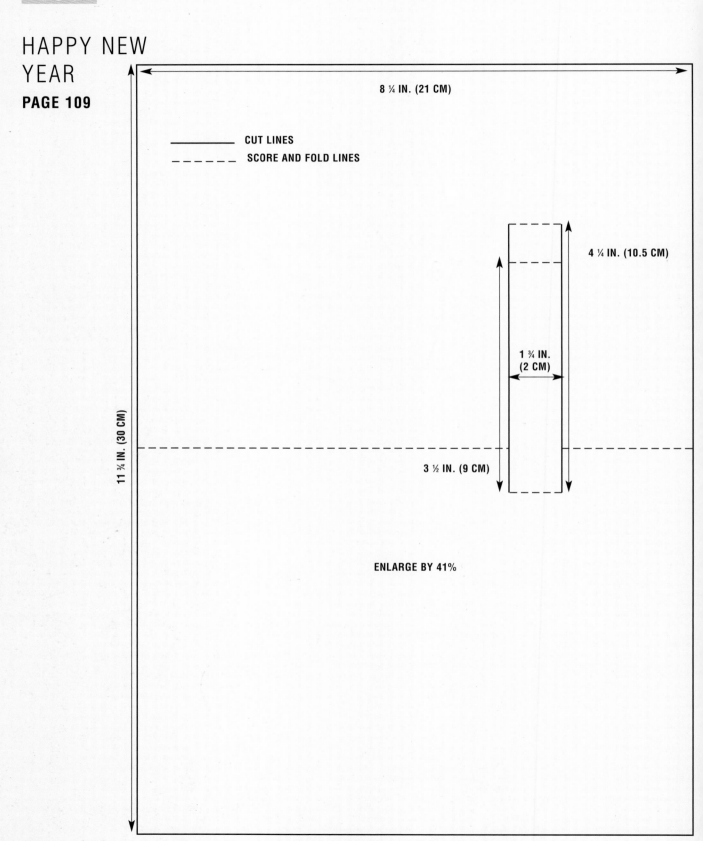

8 ¼ IN. (21 CM)

—————— **CUT LINES**

- - - - - - **SCORE AND FOLD LINES**

4 ¼ IN. (10.5 CM)

1 ¾ IN. (2 CM)

11 ¾ IN. (30 CM)

3 ½ IN. (9 CM)

ENLARGE BY 41%

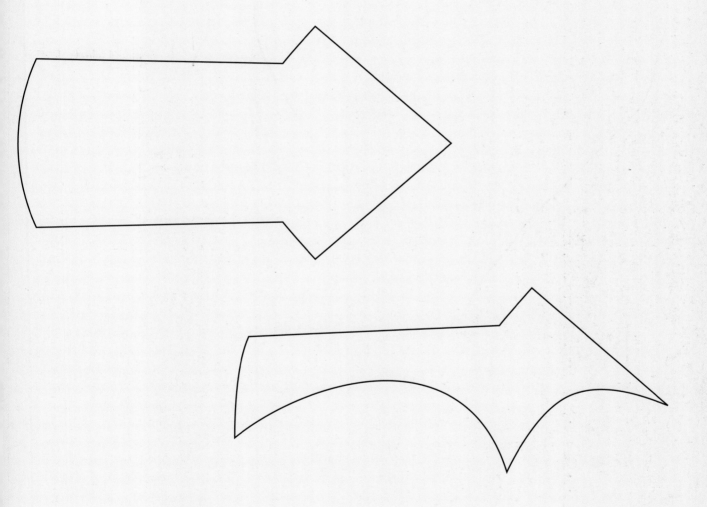

BE MY VALENTINE
PAGE 114

BEWARE THE WITCHING HOUR
PAGE 130

WINTER WARMER
PAGE 140

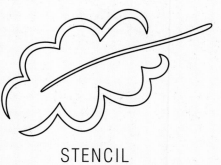

STENCIL

Index

Page numbers in *italic* refer to illustrations. As many papercraft and card-making materials and techniques are used throughout the book, the page references are intended to direct the reader to substantial entries only.

Acknowledgments

Breslich & Foss Ltd. and Lynne Garner

would like to thank the following individuals for their

help in the creation of this book:

Stephen Dew for the templates

Elizabeth Healey for designing the book

Sarah Hoggett for copy-editing the text

Janet Ravenscroft for project management

Shona Wood for the photographs

Mum and **Trudi** for the loan of craft tools and the

supply of card-making materials just when they were

needed.